PERHAPS the most familiar image of a castaway is a bearded man on a desert island—victim of disaster at sea. Yet, at times, out of a sense of duty, men have volunteered to be cast away, or have chosen to be left in some alien land as the lesser of two evils. Sometimes, order, men have been forcibly ca and stranded.

Through the centuries, as sh tured further into the unknow.., aways found themselves on remote shores. Many perished. Others doggedly kept themselves alive until they were rescued or were able to make their way back to civilization.

From among the thousands of actual castaways, Robert Carse has selected nine men and one woman whose remarkable stories deserve to be told. Though their accounts read like fiction, they are all completely factual. In time, they range from the sixteenth to the nineteenth centuries.

Carse begins with the prototype of all castaways, Alexander Selkirk, whose solitary ordeal was immortalized (but fict-
Byron and grandfather of the poet; Sparry and Goodwin, two of Sir Walter Raleigh's crew who were cast away by their captain in Guiana; Herman Melville, who left his berth on a whaler to be stranded on a Marquesan island; Mary Bryant, who made one of the greatest small boat voyages in history; and naturalist Alfred Russel Wallace, castaway more than once but never deterred from his scientific research.

THE CASTAWAYS is an absorbing collection of nine fantastic true adventures brought to life by Robert Carse's usual crisp, authoritative prose.

THE CASTAWAYS

BOOKS by ROBERT CARSE

Novels: GREAT CIRCLE, THE BECK-
ONING WATERS, FROM THE SEA AND
THE JUNGLE, DEEP SIX, PACIFIC,
HEART'S DESIRE *and* HORIZON.
Nonfiction: THE TWILIGHT OF
SAILING SHIPS, THE SEAFARERS, THE
MOONRAKERS, RUM ROW, BLOCK-
ADE, THE AGE OF PIRACY, LIFELINE,
THERE GO THE SHIPS *and* THE UN-
CONQUERED.

THE CASTAWAYS

*A Narrative History of
Some Survivers from the
Dangers of the Sea*

By ROBERT CARSE

RAND McNALLY & COMPANY
Chicago · New York · San Francisco

The sources for the photographs appearing in this book are: Alexander Selkirk artifacts and statue, *The Century Illustrated Monthly Magazine,* July, 1899; William Dampier, National Portrait Gallery, London, England; John Byron, National Maritime Museum, Greenwich, England; Willem Barents, Rijksmuseum, Amsterdam, The Netherlands; Willem Barents in the Arctic, Gerrit de Veer, *The Three Voyages of William Barents to the Arctic Regions,* London, 1609; Herman Melville, The Berkshire Athenaeum, Pittsfield, Massachusetts; Alfred R. Wallace, 1848 and Alfred R. Wallace, 1869, Alfred Russel Wallace, *My Life: A Record of Events and Opinions,* Dodd, Mead and Company, 1905.

This is for . . .
MALCOLM REISS,
who gave me the idea

FOREWORD

~~~~~~~~~~~~~~

SAINT PAUL was the first castaway to have his misfortune reported in authentic detail. The voyage during which his ship was wrecked was described by Luke, one of the three disciples who in 60 A.D. sailed with him from Myra, a port in modern Turkey. They were aboard a small wheat-carrying ship, under guard and prisoners, Paul was headed for Rome to make an appeal to Caesar from his trial before Festus.

The shipwreck was in the middle of November after the ship had been in a weeks-long tempest in the eastern Mediterranean. The vessel grounded and broke up on Malta in heavy surf and between large rocks. The scene is given in Acts 27 of the Bible. There were 276 people aboard, "and the soldiers' counsel was to kill the prisoners, lest any of them should swim out, and escape.

"But the centurion, willing to save Paul, kept them from their purpose; and commanded that they which could swim should cast themselves first into the sea, and get to land:

"And the rest, some on boards, and some on broken pieces of the ship. And so it came to pass that they all escaped safe to land."

Paul went on to Rome from Malta. The shipwreck had done him no particular harm. He appealed vigorously to Caesar, his case was examined, and an acquittal granted.

There were, over the centuries afterward, many more accounts of castaways who were less fortunate in the busy Mediterranean or outside the Pillars of Hercules where the vast sea dragons were supposed to roam and the land contained unknown, incalculable danger. But the greatest loss ever suffered by any group of castaways was that of the Spanish seamen who survived the defeat of their Armada in 1588 by the English fleet. They had fought clear in fifty-four major ships. Then, though, driven ashore by storm or hunger, they met the Scots, and the Irish.

These were wild and savage, and without mercy. They stripped the gaunt Spaniards to the skin before they killed them. Fine swords with jewelled hilts were found much later in Scottish crofter huts, but, surprisingly, in Ulster, across the Irish Sea, something like mercy was shown. A few of the Spanish crews were kept from death; they married among the Irish. Their children took Irish names, and speech, but the castaways never forgot Spain.

Hundreds of other Spanish seamen were cast away on Bermuda when homeward-bound in the huge *plata* fleets that sailed every year from Havana. The pilots had a poor understanding of longitude, and they eased over too far and too soon to the eastward, piled the high-pooped galleons on the island coral heads. Most of the crews of the ships starved, and the English who occupied the islands took the rest prisoner.

There are countless other examples of those who in various circumstances and conditions were cast away from their vessels and landed on strange and often dangerous shores. Several of the people described in this book were not castaways in the strict sense of the word. Some were forced ashore by threats against their lives, or pressures applied by the masters of the vessels in which they sailed, or through difficulties with their shipmates. They had, at best, little choice. Land was preferable to life at sea, no matter how inhospitable that might be.

They were all in their fashion castaways. A very great deal was demanded of them before they got home. The perils of their interim existence were just as extreme as any suffered by those who in absolute desperation had left a foundering ship.

ROBERT CARSE

Shelter Island, N.Y.

CONTENTS

Illustrations

When Captain Woodes Rogers returned to England in October, 1711, from his privateer voyage of circumnavigation, he brought with him Alexander Selkirk, a former sailing master who had been cast away on a small Pacific island. Rogers wrote soon afterward of Selkirk in his A CRUISING VOYAGE ROUND THE WORLD. *This book was carefully read by Daniel Defoe. He made of it his great novel* LIFE AND ADVENTURES OF ROBINSON CRUSOE. *It was fiction quite closely based on fact. Selkirk was confused with Crusoe, then all but forgotten. There was never, of course, a real Man Friday, although the Indian, William, can be dimly seen in the background of Defoe's invention.*

ALEXANDER SELKIRK

THE CAPTAIN was very firm. Alexander Selkirk was going ashore. There was no longer any place for him in the ship. Argument was useless, and refusal meant a quick ride to the main yardarm, to be hanged by the neck. The captain was absolutely opposed to Selkirk's belief that the ship was unseaworthy, must be careened soon and thoroughly repaired, and if not she would sink, never return to England.

It was mutinous on the part of Selkirk to talk so, the captain said. He pointed toward the boat that bumped alongside in the coastal swell. He told Selkirk to get aboard. Selkirk moved without speech. There was a strong possibility that Captain Thomas Stradling was a little mad. Forty-two men of the crew of sixty-two had deserted the ship earlier in this year of 1704 and gone to the island inshore. They spent weeks gambling, swimming, and chasing seals before Stradling could wheedle them back aboard.

But, Selkirk saw, looking down into the boat from the ladder at the shipside, the captain had strangely provided well for him. The boat carried his personal gear and various articles that Stradling had supplied. The men of the boat crew spoke about that on the way in to the beach from the *Cinque Ports*.

Selkirk had been sailing master aboard the ship and second in command of her. They had been in the battle together last month against the big French privateer. For seven hours, their ship, miserable old *Cinque Ports*, and William Dampier's ship, *St. George*, fought her shot for shot. But the French ship had been too powerful for them, and after she broke clear from their grapnels and sailed north along the coast, she was still in good shape.

Not so for *Cinque Ports*, though. She had been badly holed in the battle. That was the start of Selkirk's trouble with Stradling. He had told the daft loon the night of the battle that the ship would soon sink, and to leave her while there was still time.

Now, approaching the curve of the island beach, the coxswain said that if Mr. Selkirk lacked a thing or two, the boat could come in again after dark. Selkirk thanked the coxswain. He said that he believed he would make out all right as he was.

The men put him and the gear on the beach. Then they shook hands, and touched their forelocks, wished him luck. Selkirk was thirty years old. He had been seagoing most of his life. This show of respect deeply touched him, but he could not forget his distrust of Stradling.

The sun had begun to set brilliantly above the Pacific sweep, and Selkirk saw Captain Stradling in silhouette upon the quarterdeck of *Cinque Ports*. He told the men it was time they left him. The captain watched them carefully through the long glass.

Selkirk stood on the beach while the boat worked past the rollers into open water. The coxswain, crouched at the steering oar, turned and waved, and Selkirk waved back. Darkness was suddenly over the sea. He could no longer watch the boat. He picked up his gear and started to move inshore. The name of the island was Juan Fernandez, he remembered, and the Spaniards owned it.

He cursed Stradling by name, in bitter, fierce Scottish phrases. He was a sailing master, a senior officer. For no good reason should he be cast away off the coast of Chile. Like it or not, too, he was afraid. Hundreds of rats were in front of him, beyond the high tide mark on the beach. They had left leaky, foul old vessels like *Cinque Ports* and swum ashore, and here they waited for him.

Selkirk took the musket in one hand, the hatchet in the other. He walked forward. The rats scuttered ahead of him, chattering, rustling, ready to attack, and close.

The ground here was familiar to him, though. He had been on the island several times quite recently, in charge of ship's work parties that had gathered firewood and filled water casks. Men out of other vessels had also come up often from the beach, and worn a shallow trail. Selkirk followed it between the big cottonwood and pimiento trees and the groves of cabbage palms. It was the fallen coconuts from the palms that fed the rats, he knew. But he must stop somewhere.

He chose a spot over the first rise of the slope, beyond sight of the beach. The real danger for him was capture by the Spaniards or their French allies. If he was caught by them, he could expect worse treatment than that promised him by Captain Stradling. The Spaniards used the various and terrible tools of the Inquisition on their heretical English enemies, and the fact that he was an agnostic and a Scot would make no difference at all.

Stars had come clear above the ridge. Selkirk looked closely around him, trying to decide how he would best protect himself. The trees gave shelter. Before he was spotted from the beach, he would be off, upslope, needs be as far away as the high main ridge of the island.

Part of his knowledge of Juan Fernandez was that the Spaniards, angry because of the way crews from passing ships took the island goats for meat, had once brought savage dogs ashore. But the dogs died of starvation along the lower slopes, while the goats kept to the top ridges and flourished. Better to join a flock of goats, Selkirk told himself, than meet the Inquisition torturers in Lima.

He put down his musket and with the hatchet cut wood for a fire from a wind-tumbled pimiento. Then, in the way he had learned from buccaneers who had been his shipmates, he chafed a piece of the dry, soft wood against another. The friction created bright and pungent flame, and he knelt relieved next to the fire, for the rats drew back.

He went to the beach and brought to the firelight his clothing, his mathematical books and navigation instruments, his bedding, a Bible, a pound of powder, several pounds of shot, a knife, a kettle, a hammer, and a saw. The Bible and the powder and shot and the other articles had been given him through some incalculable quirk of Stradling's nature.

Selkirk stretched out beside the fire, his back against the bedding roll. Red rows of eyes peered at him in the firelight. There was a constant, small rustling as more rats congregated. If he fell asleep, Selkirk realized, they would attack his hands and his feet, his throat and his eyes.

He sat upright, completely awake. A new sound was off in the night beyond the perimeter of the firelight. He recognized that. It was made by cats. He stood and called to the cats in his most pleasant voice, used terms of endearment he recalled from his boyhood at home in Fifeshire.

When the cats did not respond he became quite desperate. He grabbed his musket and leaped forth among the rats, killing with wide swipes of the iron-shod butt. The hatchet as he flung it finished more, and afterward the cats advanced to him. He fed the carcasses to the cats, caressed those who were not too wild.

But sleep suddenly seized him. He staggered where he stood among the scores of cats. It was difficult to gather enough wood to keep the fire going for the night. He slumped down against the bedding roll, the musket and the hatchet under his outflung arms, and slept.

He awoke before dawn, lay very still. The pattering rustle of the rats diminished and then was gone as he moved. The thick soles of his boots had been chewed from heel to toe. His new-found friends, the cats, had not kept a thorough watch. He must build himself a hut where he could stay safe from the rats. Else, as they grew bolder, they would surely kill him.

Selkirk hid his belongings in the branches of a big cottonwood tree, then started for the top of the island. He wanted to explore all of it, and get to know it well. Most anybody coming here would be his enemy; he should know every possible way of escape to the ridges.

He walked fast, feeling alert and confident, but very hungry. He carried the musket loaded, primed, brought it to his shoulder when the long, yellow grass before him stirred. That could be a goat, and the makings of several meals. Then he laughed. A pair of scrawny cats emerged from the grass, chewing on what was left of some small bird, and looking at him with open appeal.

"So I'm to feed ye," he said. He was glad to break the silence; after many months in a small, crowded ship, it had begun to oppress him. "How about ye takin' me to the goats, though? Whither away might they be?"

The cats turned. They disappeared in the grass and, almost without conscious thought, he followed. He was from Largo, he told himself, his youth spent in the village or at sea, and not in the Highlands. This was all new to him. He was no hunter, except that serving aboard the privateers he had learned to shoot a musket straight.

The cats went up one ridge and then another, and a third. The sun was hot. Selkirk panted in his heavy coat and britches and his woolen stockings. He needed a drink of water, and the hunger made him ache. The goat he saw was too far away for a certain shot, still he tried it.

"Ye're lucky, lad," he said.

The goat had been on the next ridge and about to scramble over it. The bullet struck right behind the shoulder, and the goat sprang only once, gave a final, short bleat.

Selkirk was too hungry to carry the goat far. He made a fire and swiftly stripped the hide and butchered while the pair of cats nudged him. They ate together, and Selkirk found names for them, Starboard and Larboard. He wrapped what remained of the meat in the hide, kept on toward the top ridge.

No other goats came within range although he saw a number during the rest of his march. They had been hunted often enough before, he thought, and it would take fair skill on his part and a great lot of running to hunt them. But his lungs were good, his legs, too, and he should be able to take care of himself here.

He sat for some time on the top ridge, feeling a great sense of loneliness, and very sorry for himself. The only reason for his trouble with Stradling had been that he owned the courage to speak out and tell the man *Cinque Ports* was unseaworthy. The other officers kept their mouths shut. The canny kind, that was what they were. When they were alone with him, they called him Sawney, in affection, but when Stradling came close, they left him, and again he was Mister Selkirk. So, let them sink with the ship, and let him be done with the past.

Selkirk stood erect, a husky, broad-shouldered man in his knee-length blue coat, his wide britches, the wind from off the sea sharply against him. That was the prevailing wind which blew, he told himself, and kept steadily out of the southward. The Spanish mainland, Chile, was off to the east, and beyond to the west was nothing but the huge emptiness of the Pacific.

The island was small, perhaps half a dozen miles long. It was a thousand and some feet tall on this ridge, and there were two bays, one below him on the Pacific side, the other at the northwesterly end. The position for it on the chart was 34° 10′ South latitude, he knew, although he had forgotten the longitude. That was something for him to work out, and he had plenty else to keep him busy.

"Get ye doon, Sawney," he said. The cats stared at him as he spoke, and he was pleased by that. It was quite likely that he would be here a long time. How long he had no way of reckoning. But he must keep his wits, and a bit of talk to himself did more good than harm.

He started the hut the next morning, building close to the site of his original camp. He trimmed logs from the pimiento wood, raised a fair-sized hut with two side windows and a doorway. For thatch, he used the long, coarse grass that grew in profusion over most of the island. He wove it, secured it with withes, covered both the walls and the rough plank roof. His almost daily hunting brought him a number of goatskins, and he pegged those out beyond reach of the rats, stretched and cured them, later stitched them together and lined the interior of the hut.

It was reasonably weatherproof, he found, and he went ahead and built shelves, a stool, and a table. He had since the first day kept a calendar on a piece of board, with marks for each day in regular columns. The date of his arrival here, October 2, 1704, was cut deeply into the bark of a tree. Despite the calendar and the reminder on the tree, the days began to blur together in his mind.

The solitude pressed upon him with terrible weight, nearly crushed his ability to think. The days were all very much alike, the weather fair with only occasional rain squalls. He walked the beach until he knew every little indentation, cove, and inlet. He fished with hooks fashioned from pieces of rusted iron discovered in rotted planks at high tide level, and with line made from palm coir.

But the fish diet gave him dysentery. He lost his appetite, failed to eat until he was so weak he could hardly tend the fire and make himself goat meat broth. Then he went to the beach and gathered crawfish that were as big as lobsters. He boiled them in sea water or broiled them over his fire as his appetite returned. Turnips grew wild on the island from a garden started by two men from an English buccaneer crew cast away here last year. The meat of the coconut from the cabbage palm, shredded and dipped in some of the fermented milk, was another dish he came to like.

He ate it with the inevitable boiled, broiled, or stewed goat meat. A pepper he made from the grated pimiento helped the taste, and had a delicious tang and smell. Then he found another black pepper which he knew the Spanish on this coast called *malagita,* and he began to forget that he lacked salt, and bread.

He built a second, smaller hut in which he kept his tools. When his coat and britches wore out from running through the brush on the high ridges after goats, he made himself new clothing. It was something to occupy the time, he told himself. Back in Largo his father had been the village shoemaker. Some of that skill should have come along to him.

He measured goat hides, sharpened an awl and a needle, used thread that came from an old pair of worsted stockings. The needle was designed to sew sail canvas, and he was forced to work slowly or he would break it. The garments took weeks before he was finished, but then they fitted him quite well. He was elated. His shirts were worn-out, and he took some of his very small supply of linen, sewed himself a new pair.

This he considered to be a real triumph, and at dusk he tossed a lot of wood onto the fire, roasted a goat and some crawfish, cooked a mess of turnips. He ate sitting cross-legged beside the fire, his favorite cats near him, the rest a few paces away with the younger goats he had gradually tamed. His feud with the rats was about finished; he had killed many of them, and now a legion of about a hundred cats helped protect him.

He rose to his feet at the end of the meal and gave the meat scraps to the cats, the leftover vegetables to the goats. He added a couple of handfuls of raw turnips for the goats, and the young kids among them scampered happily and nudged him. They wanted him to dance, he realized.

"Verra well," he said. "And so I will!"

His hands on his hips, he began to whistle a jig, stamped his feet in time, then danced. The animals danced

with him, in and out of the firelight, and they tried faithfully
to follow the steps as he changed from strathspeys to reels
and Highland flings. His breath came short at last; he stood
motionless, looking down at his feet.

They were bare, calloused, and misshapen. Weeks ago,
upon the rocky ridges, the soles of his boots had torn apart
in useless strips of battered leather. There was no way of
making new. He lacked the heavy leather. And him with his
father a shoemaker.

Selkirk laughed. But the sound was forced. He sat down
on the ground and held his head in his hands. "Your lad's not
doing unco gude," he said. He spoke as if to his father and
mother, and there in Largo they could hear him. "'Tis sore
bad, being so lonely. Aye. Your Sawney misses you."

Sawney was his family nickname, and to say it gave him
some small sense of comfort. He had the feeling that somehow, mysteriously, his parents were in communication with
him. His mother might pray for him. He was not the religious
kind; the elders of the church in Largo had chased him out
for what they said was indecency. They blamed him for
unduly fighting with his brothers. The sour-bellied old lot
had nearly broken his mother's heart with that. But there in
the hut he had a Bible, and he could read from it as well as
the next man.

Selkirk went into the hut and got the Bible. He put wood
on the fire and roused the flame, then read long passages
aloud while the cats stared at him and the goats slumped
down asleep. When his eyes were tired he put the Bible back.
The mood of depression was gone. He felt considerably
better. There were small black plums to be picked up on the
high ridges, he remembered, and they had a fine taste. Then,
in June and until September, the sea lions would be ashore

by the hundreds on the beaches. The seals would come later, in November.

There would be plenty to keep him busy, and all the fresh meat he could eat. "Don't be too sorry for yourself," he said. He had just remembered that other men had been marooned or cast away here for long periods of time. The sailor who was named William and was an Indian from the Mosquito tribe had been alone on the island during a stay of several years, and had come off it in fair enough shape.

"You can do the same," Selkirk muttered. "So get to sleep!"

He remembered in the morning all that he had heard about William. His pride was piqued. If a Mosquito Indian could do well here, then he must, too. He was a poor sort if he failed, and would never be able to go back to Largo.

The story was that William had been left on the island in 1681 by Captain Watling. There was a falling out between the masters of the buccaneer ships that raided the coast, and Watling suddenly decided to sail. William was out in the woods hunting goats when the ship hauled anchor. He was alone. All he had was his musket, powder and shot, and a knife.

He got in a good supply of meat before his ammunition was finished. Then he sawed the gun barrel into small pieces. He used them for harpoon heads, lance points, and fish hooks. His hut was built of pimiento wood, thatched with grass, and lined with goatskins.

Come to think of it, Selkirk told himself, he had followed William's style a good deal around here. The Indian had also made clothing out of goatskin when his other gear was gone. Then, in 1684, a pair of English privateer ships under Captain Davis' command went to anchor off the Pacific-side beach. There was a sailor aboard one of them named Robin, and he was from the Mosquito tribe, the same as William.

He asked permission and went ashore first and met William. They came back out to Davis' ship. William said he wanted to sail some more. So Davis put him on articles with the rest of the crew, and when the ships had taken wood and water they shoved off up the coast.

Selkirk wondered if William had ever been as lonely as he was. He'd like to talk with William some time and find out. Och, aye, he'd just like to talk and be listened to by a human being. The wind sound was so familiar it pulled at his nerves, and the cats and the kids must think him daft, listened to him only because he fed them.

Selkirk stood ready to go up the ridge and gather the wild plums that would make a fine sauce for his meat. He carried the musket, powder and shot, and a goatskin sack for the plums. But he did not start toward the high land. He turned around and walked down to the beach.

His extremely sensitized hearing had told him that a ship was offshore. He heard the rattle of a wooden block as it was put to strain, and the squeal of the sheave as a halyard was brought taut. He ran open-mouthed, panting with excitement and, in the moment of initial shock, careless about discovery.

Then he moved cautiously, keeping to the underbrush, crawling from tree to tree. But he was frantic with his desire to make contact with people. His throat cords trembled; his lips worked, and he formed sentences which he would use to introduce himself, explain his presence on the island.

The ship was of about five hundred tons, her hull sea-chafed, her sails green with the mildew from weeks of Cape Horn wet. She was a French brig, Selkirk told himself, and probably a privateer brought to the coast to capture English ships.

Selkirk lay down behind the bole of a cabbage palm a few yards above the beach. He propped the musket beside him, made sure it was loaded. But, he told himself, there were good folks among the French. Not all of them worked hand in hand with the Spaniards and would send a man to the Inquisitors just because a crazy captain had cast him away on this island. This crew in particular, they'd let him go, they would, and have a real good talk, and see he got some brandy, and tobacco, and a pipe.

He spoke several French phrases, and knew they sounded strange with his Largo accent. He should bow, he told himself, and say to the captain that he was the Frenchman's obedient servant for life.

The brig had just backed her mainsail and come up into the wind to anchor. Selkirk clearly heard the hail upon the wind and understood it. The French captain was telling his mate to drop the anchor.

Spume made a rainbow cascade around the anchor. The ship fetched up, took her scope, lay still. A boat was being swung out and lowered. Men climbed into it. Some of them had muskets, Selkirk saw, and all had cutlasses. Sweat ran down the backs of his hands and dropped from his fingertips onto the grass. He gulped with his effort to keep from shouting. He must wait, he knew, for the boat to reach the beach.

It helped him to look at the birds. The tension was released a little, and the passage of the minutes became bearable. He identified red-breasted blackbirds, and humming birds of various colors that were as small as bees, swept in fast spirals above the grass. Gulls rode the crests of the rollers offshore, and tern marched stiff-legged but dainty along the sand.

The boat was in the rollers, through them, and about to ground. The bowman leaped out and took the painter, began to haul. The officer who sat in the stern beside the coxswain gave a sharp order. All of the oarsmen left the boat, and the coxswain, and the officer. The officer advanced onto the beach, his tricorne hat low against the sun, his eyes squinted.

Now, Selkirk thought. He got to his feet, leaving the musket in the grass. He lifted his hands to show that they were empty. Then he said that he was a castaway, and he wished the Frenchmen good day.

The officer fired the pistol so fast that Selkirk saw only the yellow flash. He heard the drubbing of the bullet past his head and the flat report as he started to duck. Then he grasped the musket and ran. Half a dozen of the Frenchmen were firing at him with pistols and muskets. He cursed them, but he did not stop. It would make no sense if he fired back, he realized. That would be a matter of pride alone, and probably get him killed. And he needed all his ammunition. From the looks of this, he was going to be on the island much longer than he had thought when the fears rode him the worst.

The Frenchmen were gone when he came back from the highest ridge. He had watched with hatred and vast longing while the boat returned to the ship. He could make out even from that distance that she was low in the water. Her water casks were filled from the same spring he used, he told himself, and the boat loaded to the gunwales with wood he had chopped. Damn them, the frog-eating tinkers!

But when he reached his camp he found nothing gone except a couple of coconuts. They had been in his sleeping hut all right, the Frenchmen. He could see their boot marks outside, and they had examined all of his tools and equipment. He felt perverse anger. They should have taken something of value. This way, they showed pity for him.

He walked up and down between the huts, cursing in a wild voice. He told himself that he was glad he had fought in the battle against the big French privateer. Selkirk beat his fists together in frustration. He cursed Captain Stradling. But it did no good, he recognized, and the sound of the words bored him, had lost their effect.

He should do something—must do something—to keep his sanity. It was all too easy to walk out there from the beach, wade deep, and keep right on, following the sunset into the West.

He picked up a goatskin sack, took a staff, called his favorite cats, and went toward the high ground to pick plums. This was the eighth month he was here. Next month was June, and he'd be hunting the sea lions. That would hold him busy till September and the seal-hunting time.

So now it was plums. And when he had his share of them, he'd go hunting goats. It was a good idea for him to make a full count of the entire lot on the island. Slit their ears as a mark and keep a record.

He plucked and stewed plums until he had no more containers in which to keep the stuff. Then the sea lions were ashore. They were a stupid but dangerous prey; some of the males were more than twenty feet long and weighed a ton. He hunted them with a harpoon, stepping delicately along the beach while they swayed around him, the broad, lion-like heads lifted, the wide whiskers shiny, and the red-rimmed small eyes fixed upon him with an uncomprehending stare.

Selkirk remembered that some men with whom he had been shipmates were bold enough to thrust a pistol into a sea lion's mouth, aim down the throat, and then pull the trigger. There were others who preferred what they called "lion baiting." They took half-pikes and prodded, stabbed, shoved, sent the mammals floundering, bloody out into the sea to drown from exhaustion.

Selkirk killed for the meat and the hides with their coarse, thick hair. He might use those for clothing, or for the hull covering of a boat when he was ready to leave here. Anyhow, he got no pleasure from idle slaughter of the dumb brutes. He told himself this proudly, and gave up the hunting. He would wait for the smarter, rougher lot, the young male seals, before he came back here to the beach.

Selkirk began to run the high ridges every day. He wore nothing except his knee-long britches. His hair had grown almost down to his shoulders and he had hacked it off with his knife. It clustered thickly around his ears, joined with his beard. He had made himself a conical cap of goatskin, and wore it against the sun. He had been too long alone now to have any idea of his appearance and was wholly unselfconscious. When he went to the ridges at dawn, he carried the musket, his powder horn and shotbag, and his new knife. The old knife had worn through to the back of the blade, and he had taken a piece of iron found on the beach and fashioned it into another.

Running the ridges fascinated him. The wind and the sunlight played upon him, and he was exhilarated. His strength, his speed of foot, his keenness of vision intoxicated him. He could run faster than the fastest goat. He was alone, surely so. But he, Alexander Selkirk, once of Largo, in the ancient kingdom of Fife, presently of Juan Fernandez Island, in the South Sea, and rich in memory and hope, was the king of the island.

He chased a swift-footed goat for hours one day, leaping, swerving among underbrush and rocks and close to deep gorges. His pride had become so intense that he would not use the musket. This beastie he would catch with his hands, and only for mercy's sake use the knife to slit the gullet.

But, running hard, his hands out to grasp the goat by the horns, he went forth into space. He dived with his hands still tensed to grasp the horns, and his legs in motion. The sky flashed. He screamed, and kept on going, over, over. Over once more, and then he struck.

He came to consciousness with the sun in his eyes. Then, gradually, his senses registered. He felt the goat under him. The goat was dead. Selkirk moved, filled with pain. He got clear of the carcass and submitted to the pain, but told himself that he must have been here for at least twenty-four hours.

His musket was several yards away in the brush that had saved his life. The powder horn and shotbag had been lost in flight. He rose up on his hands and knees and began to crawl.

It was about a mile to the camp. He came to it weeping and in delirium with the cats around him, bending down and startled. But the young kids stayed away; he had enough sense left to understand that they were repelled by the smell of the carcass that clung heavily to him.

He remembered later that he stayed in the hut for ten days, inert, lassitudinous, the pain a dark cloud that kept him from clear thought. The pain retreated, and he drank broth, ate some of his stewed plums, got back a bit of strength. He stood with the help of a staff, then went to recover his musket, found the goat's carcass stripped by gulls and rats.

He stayed away from the ridges when his strength returned. That was because of fear, he knew. And now the seals were on the island. They jammed the beaches to make love, and whelp. The males were a challenge to him. They kept a day and night chorus, and the females joined them. Selkirk could not sleep. The bleating, the barking, the roaring excited his stifled sexual instinct. He went to the beaches in wild jealousy, and fought and killed the young males.

They were about six feet in length, scarred and defiant; they had already fought the older males for the females. When Selkirk strode toward them howling challenge the older males reared up from the shallows where they had been driven and hopefully watched. Selkirk killed wantonly, using a heavy club. His mind was possessed by a swirl of confused, erotic images.

He was hardly aware of the risks he took, and the blood that splashed him, the fatigue that reached from his arms through all his body. He saw instead of the blunt, brown heads, the yellow fangs and protuberant, fear-blurred eyes, the faces of the women he had known. They were from his home village, or from Grangemouth, or Leith, or Aberdeen, and some from ports overseas. Those foreign ones were tavern lasses, wild in their actions, and bold.

Selkirk walked away from the beach when he was too tired to kill. He smelled of death, he realized. The cats kept away from him; the kids had disappeared into the underbrush. He made a fire in the fireplace before his hut, meaning to heat some broth, but he was not hungry.

He felt oddly empty and spent, and a little sick. This was different from having been with a woman, he thought. He had done something to himself, inside. He was dirty there. He should never have killed so many of the poor, brute seals. "Pray, sinner," he said. "Then read a chapter from the gude book."

He got out the Bible after he had prayed, poked up the fire, and read by its light for hours. That calmed him and made him feel that his life could be bearable. He recited the Psalms. He sang hymns from memory, improvising verses that he had forgotten. When his voice was hoarse and he could not sing any more, he recalled that he had been forced to leave home because of trouble with the elders of the church.

Selkirk laughed at the memory. He was a better Christian now than he had ever been in Largo. That would please the elders—damn their narrow, tight, and dark souls.

Selkirk took off his clothing, crusted stiff with seal blood. He washed himself carefully at the spring, rubbed his body clean with handfuls of leaves. Then he put on fresh clothing, left the soiled garments to soak in one of the buckets he had made. It was broad daylight, and yet he found that he was very sleepy.

He had cleansed himself inside, too, he thought. For the rest of his stay here, he would be all right. But he must keep on reading the Bible. It steadied him. And if at any time he got bored by it, he had his navigation books to study and problems to work. He still didn't know the exact longitude of the island.

He lived in an almost dreamlike existence after that, for considerable periods actually lost in trance. He sat on the high ridges during late afternoon and sank into a rapture of the senses. The sun was marvelously warm upon his skin. The breeze from off the southern ocean was just cool enough to be pleasant. It carried to him the faint, spicy tang of the pimiento trees, and the slow splash and retreat of the rollers. Out upon the western horizon the enormous bronze and gold masses of cumulus cloud gathered. They were like mountains that rose out of the air itself.

Their valleys were the blue of bluebells, some of the slopes the same shade as the purple heather, and others a thistle pink, and rose, and lavender. When the colors faded, it was as though darkness lifted from the ocean floor, swiftly closed upon the last of the light.

Selkirk went down from the high ground in darkness. He walked the main, westward beach, waiting for the starlight. He sat neck deep in the sea when the stars were overhead. There was very little tide, and the water gently lapped him as he looked aloft and named the stars and their constellations.

A great peace held him. This was his world. He kept it without blemish. He had never felt such calm, such ease of spirit aboard any ship or in any other place. Aye, not even in Largo.

But then he had been on the island for four years. He became very disturbed the morning he carved the date on his calendar. Something was badly wrong with him, he thought. He could not go on drifting like this. He was about to lose his hold on life, forget who he was, and where he was.

He started that day to build beacons at various points around the island. He made them of dry logs and heaped them high, so that when he set them aflame their glare would carry for miles to seaward. There was, of course, always the chance that the crew of the ship that saw his beacons would be Spanish or French. Still, the chance must be taken. Alexander Selkirk had been king of the island too long. He was very near becoming a slack-mouthed idiot.

The pair of ships showed their topsails over the southwesterly horizon. He saw them from the highest ridge where he had gone to keep count of the goat herds. He stared at the ships breathless and motionless. They bore down on the island; they steered a course for here, would anchor offshore.

He ran full tilt down the slopes to the hut. This was it, he thought. He could not delay any longer. He looked at the calendar. Four years and four months. Time enough.

He took the musket, the powder horn and shotbag, but as he ran toward the nearest beacon he told himself that they would be of no use to him. There'd be no more waiting. He'd take his chances of capture. Selkirk was leaving the island if the men in those ships would have him.

Both ships were at anchor when he reached the beacon. They looked to be English-built, but there was no way to be sure, what with the way vessels changed flags in the war. One of them, he saw, was swinging out her pinnace. That would head for the beach. Her crew had stowed water casks and axes in her. They were what was called a waterers and wooders party.

Selkirk knelt down beside the beacon. He sprinkled powder among the dry branches at the bottom. Then he pulled the trigger of the musket and the flintlock spark leaped to the powder. The fire burned with a high, orange flame. But he heaped on more wood, and waved and yelled to the men in the boat.

The boat crew were resting on their oars. Their officer stood erect with the afternoon sun at his back and examined the beach. Then he sat down again and took the tiller and gestured. The boat swung and went back to the ship.

Selkirk stood by the beacon fire with his eyes shut. He could not look at the boat. It was unbelievable that she had not landed. But he could hear along the breeze the sounds that were made as she came alongside the ship, and the falls were hooked on, and she was hoisted from the water. There were bits of speech he heard, too, and they sounded like English.

He stayed all night beside the beacon. He could not bring himself to leave it. The ships were English, he told himself. A boat would be in again in the morning. One captain or the other would decide that this fire wasn't some sort of Spanish trick for an ambush.

The dawn was gray, then blue and crimson. The sun shone broadly over the sea. Selkirk gazed bleary-eyed at the ships; he saw the smoke from the galleys and believed he could hear the cooks calling the men to breakfast. Pretty soon now, if it was to happen at all, a boat would pull for shore.

He walked to the beach with slow, measured strides. He had left the musket behind him at the beacon. This time, the boat must not turn back. It was a yawl which came in with the landward breeze. She was well-handled, and jib, main, and mizzen drew full.

Selkirk waded out knee-deep into the rollers. He tried his voice. It was very hoarse. He should wait until the boat was quite close. Then he would speak clear and plain, and only in English.

The yawl sheered off, though. She went on the other tack and continued on along the coast of the island toward the northerly side. Selkirk stood gazing at her until she was out of sight around the curve of the beach. He was silent. Grief gripped him so hard that he was beyond coherent thought.

Then he looked up, the tears across his vision, and there was the other boat. He recognized her. She was the pinnace he had seen yesterday. Six men were at her oars now, and two officers sat in the sternsheets. They were armed. He saw the cutlasses, the muskets, and the pistols. He moved, and very slowly waved his arms.

One of the officers saw him. He pointed. The other officer nodded and gave an order to the men at the oars. The pinnace changed course. She was steered directly toward Selkirk.

Selkirk stopped waving. He stood still, the rollers around his knees in a quick little rush and slower ebb. The oarsmen were staring at him over their shoulders, and the officers had drawn and lifted pistols. The senior officer, a big, red-faced man, shouted, "Who are you, m' lad? Speak up!"

"Selkirk," he said in a thick voice. He wanted to weep and was already beginning to sob. "Alexander Selkirk. Sailing master out of the *Cinque Ports*. Been here four years and more."

He was saved, he knew. These men were English. The impulse to weep was gone. He felt instead a sense of shock. It was going to be very hard to leave the island.

The red-faced man said that he was Captain Thomas Dover. The other, younger officer was Mr. Frye. They both stared curiously at Selkirk and he understood that they did not mean to be rude. But it was only when he saw one of the sailors laughing that he realized how strange he must seem. His whiskers were as long as any goat's, and his hair was down to his shoulders again.

Then Captain Dover suddenly spoke and asked him if there were crawfish to be found along the beach. Selkirk nodded, and started to run along the beach. But he ran so fast that they could not catch up to him, and he was relieved. He wanted to be alone for a few minutes more.

He wanted to say good-bye to the island. His cats and the kids were scattering off into the brush, afraid of these people behind him. Selkirk gestured to the pets. He called softly in farewell.

When the boat left the island she went to the ship named *Duke*. She was about 300 tons, Selkirk reckoned, and mounted thirty guns. The other ship was named *Duchess*. She was smaller and carried twenty-six guns. Both ships mustered more than a hundred men, from the count he made as they gathered along the bulwarks and gaped at him.

He looked back calmly enough, interested in the ships and their condition. This was a privateer venture, he told himself. But the men did not yell at him, or jostle each other. There were marines in smart uniforms at the ladder-heads. He was glad that he noticed the degree of discipline. He was after all a castaway, lacking any sort of discharge. He would have to explain several things.

Captain Dover had grabbed the rope ladder, was bumping up it. He waved to Selkirk to follow him.

Selkirk had been waiting for the younger officer, Mr. Frye, but now he climbed rapidly onto deck.

The marine sentries stood with grounded muskets, expressionless. He turned aft and saw that Captain Dover moved toward the quarterdeck. He allowed Dover to get three paces ahead; that was a good, respectful distance.

Selkirk was trying very hard to decide what he should say about his stay on the island. The fact that he had been in a bitter argument with his former captain would make a pretty poor impression on the commander of this venture. He went up the quarterdeck ladder with reluctant strides.

Captain Dover stood beside a keen-faced, slender man who wore a bag wig, a high stock, and the unmistakable expression of authority. The slender man, after Dover had named Selkirk and explained that he claimed to be the former sailing master of *Cinque Ports*, gave Selkirk a sharp glance. Then he said that he was Woodes Rogers, the master of this vessel. But, Dover said importantly, he was the captain of the marine detachment and president of the council of officers. He told Selkirk to speak up, and enough of this standing here in silence.

But Selkirk stayed silent. Words were very difficult for him to pronounce. The island solitude was a barrier between him and these men. He had changed; he had lost his power of speech. But he must speak, he realized, and slowly told Rogers about the argument with Stradling and why he had left *Cinque Ports*.

Selkirk fell back into the broad Fifeshire accent of his youth. He spoke brokenly, with a harsh defiance and pride.

This should be told straight, he decided. Let the men here make up their minds about him after they had heard the worst of it, not just his version alone.

Captain Rogers was smiling. He motioned at Selkirk. Both he and Dover were West of England men, he said. But they could not fathom all his Scot's talk. Selkirk had better try plain English.

Selkirk was sweating. His hands trembled. This pair, he thought, could send him back to the island if they wanted. They did not have to keep him in the ship. But they had turned around toward the companionway hatch. The man who came from it was William Dampier.

Dampier called Selkirk by his nickname of Sawney, and gripped him hard by the hand. Selkirk laughed with joy. Dampier was his old friend, had been master of a ship that accompanied *Cinque Ports* on the last voyage. He knew all about the battle against the French, and how badly *Cinque Ports* was hurt.

Now Dampier looked at Selkirk with concern. He cursed Stradling, and said that Selkirk should never have been cast away here.

Selkirk shrugged. The joy of recognition had gone out of him. He again felt alien. He wondered what authority Dampier had in this ship. Dampier had served for years as a buccaneer, raided in the Spanish Main and here along the South American coast. Back in London, and with men like Rogers and Dover he might count for very little.

But Woodes Rogers sensed Selkirk's thought. He said that they knew all about Dampier. The old rogue was also without doubt the best pilot and cartographer alive. He served as pilot in this ship. Captain Dover and Rogers had great faith in him.

Dover said that when the expedition was finished with

the Spaniards, Dampier would take the expedition around the world on the way home.

Dampier grunted as he listened. He told Selkirk that *Cinque Ports* had foundered off the Costa Rican coast. Only six or seven men, Stradling among them, got out of her. The Spaniards captured the lot and they were presently under the Inquisition torture at Lima.

Dampier looked at Woodes Rogers. He asked the captain if the expedition needed a sailing master.

There would be such a need, Rogers said, as soon as a ship was seized from the Spaniards. The job would go to Selkirk. Meanwhile, Dampier would find him quarters, food, and new gear.

Selkirk was able to laugh as he thanked Rogers. He would keep his goatskin clothing, he said, until he had the chance to show the island to the people in these ships. They might want some of the meat that came along with the skins.

The length of the speech amazed him, and he knew that he was tempted to go on talking for hours, spill out all that the solitude had kept pent up in him. But Dampier understood; the old buccaneer had been often with other returned castaways. Dampier led him below to the main cabin. He told Selkirk to sit down and relax.

Selkirk sat motionless on the bench. He was nearly overcome by the sights, the sounds, and the smells of the vessel. He had forgotten during the island years how much of a sailor he was. His heart was here, in a well-kept vessel like this, the sunlight aglitter in reflection from the sea and casting broad beams through the colored glass of the stern gallery windows. He heard the sharp insistence of a pipe as a bosun's mate gave an order to the watch; there were the odors of oakum and tar, hemp, canvas, and freshly washed wood.

Dampier came back with two pewter pots of beer. The

stuff was bitter, unfamiliar to Selkirk, and he drank slowly while Dampier talked and told him of the expedition. All of the rich bigwigs in Bristol backed the voyage, had seen that the ships were equipped with privateer commissions from the king. It was all very legal.

The Spaniards, though, Selkirk said, would call them pirates.

Dampier winked at him over the rim of the beer pot. They were after Spanish loot, he said. Rogers was keen for it, and Dover, who was really a physicker, a doctor, had come off to sea to make his fortune. Dover's share in the expedition was big, and he held enough power with the owners to bring along his big brute of a bulldog. That was what Selkirk heard barking. The dog was penned up on the fo'c'sle-head. Captain Courtney, who was in command of *Duchess*, wouldn't have the dog in his ship.

Selkirk had finished the beer. He felt it along his veins and nerves. He held out the pot to Dampier. But Captain Rogers was coming down the companionway ladder from deck. He told Dampier that no more beer was to be drunk. All of the ship's company except an anchor watch was heading for the shore. There were, he said in explanation to Selkirk, a number of sick men aboard both ships. They had picked up frostbite and various injuries and sicknesses while off Cape Horn. If a camp could be found for them ashore, that would be fine. Captain Doctor Dover advocated it along with a run for his loud-lunged bulldog.

Selkirk said that he knew the exact spot for a camp on the island. It was near the beach, but among trees. Old sails or tarpaulins could be rigged as tents.

He was greatly satisfied by his answer to Rogers. His ability to speak had come back to him. He had just talked clearly, and with good sense, like an officer. Nor had his time on the island been wasted. The knowledge he had of it was a real help to the expedition.

Captain Rogers asked him if he thought there was a goat ashore that would run faster than Dover's dog. Selkirk laughed at that. He said that he could outrun any goat on the island. Then, Rogers said, a few guineas could be made in a wager. Let Will Dampier make that. Captain Dover had enormous pride in his dog and money to back up his affection.

"We're grateful," Dampier said. "I'll handle the bet. Thank you, sir."

"But get the boats away at once," Rogers said. "Tell the bosun to pipe all hands."

The sick men from both boats were rowed ashore that afternoon and a camp set up near the beach. Selkirk directed the operation. He piloted the boat through the rollers, then showed the work party how to rig the shelters. The sick made comfortable, cooking fires laid, food and fresh water handy, he agreed to race against Dover's bulldog.

Captain Rogers was insistent about the race. He had aroused Dover's vanity, Selkirk realized, and got the doctor to make a big bet with Dampier. The former buccaneer had been loud in his praise of the speed of foot of "my old friend, Sawney Selkirk." It was enough to make Dover boast about Lord Harry, the bulldog, and to offer odds of two-to-one to Dampier.

But Selkirk hardly listened to the talk. He was again remote, drawn back and away from these men. Rogers had questioned him about the island while the camp was being built. Selkirk answered him carelessly, without much thought. Rogers had from the first moment here called him "Governor." He meant it as a joke, Selkirk thought. And that was all it could be.

Selkirk was acutely aware that the island was no longer

his. Hunting parties searched the woods. There were musket reports from the high ridges. When he raced Lord Harry, he almost lost to the squat, snuff-colored dog because of lack of interest.

He looked around him as he ran, wondering which of his pets had already been killed by the hunters. Lord Harry was a full fifteen yards ahead of him on the last lap along the beach when he decided that he wanted to win. He dug his toes into the smooth, damp sand and gave a burst of speed, used the muscles that he had strengthened in daily sprints here. Across the line, while Dampier pounded his back, Rogers enthusiastically shook his hand, and Dover glared, he stood wordless. He had nothing to say. He still lived alone, deep within himself. The habit of withdrawal from the present still persisted and was a permanent part of his nature.

The expedition left the island when the sick were recovered. The ships sailed a northeast by east course, looking for booty off the mainland. They met and took a small Spanish ship and named her *Increase*. A prize crew was put aboard with Selkirk as sailing master. But he felt no particular elation because of the appointment. His thought reached back to the island. He missed solitude, and his pets.

It was decided in officers' council on April 13 that an attack was to be made on the city of Guayaquil. That was up the Guayas River from the coast. A considerable amount of danger was involved. The ships must be left at the mouth of the river where there was a seventeen-foot tide. Boats would be used, and the jungle that flanked the river was infested with snakes, mosquitoes, chiggers, and leeches. Then, at the village of Puna, below the city, a copy of a warning from the Viceroy was found. The people were warned of the arrival of a force under "the Conduct of an *Englishman* named Dampier."

Selkirk laughed when that was read aloud by Rogers. A startled look was across Dampier's gaunt face. The old buccaneer said that he was surprised to be so famous here. Rogers said that all hands would learn more about him when Guayaquil had been taken. But the Spaniards were certainly well-informed.

There was sharp action at Guayaquil. Selkirk took part in it, landed from the boats with the rest of the force and charged the Spanish cannon in the *plaza*. But he had no feeling of intense emotion or sense of danger. It was, he thought, as if his real self was on the island, and all that was here was a man who answered to his name.

But the next morning, with the city secured, Rogers sent him further up the river in command of a small scouting party. Most of the loot that the English had expected to find was hidden somewhere, and Rogers believed that the wives and daughters of the Spanish officers had taken it into the jungle.

Selkirk brought the boat around a bend in the river and on the bank beyond saw a large group of women. They stood at the edge of a savannah, and Negro slaves guarded the canoes that had carried them from the city. Selkirk understood. The women were frightened by the thought of capture but were unwilling to enter the jungle. They stood motionless in their tight, fragile dresses and stared at him and his men.

Selkirk put the boat alongside the bank. He walked forward with the sailors deployed behind him. Then he halted, quite close to the women.

They had hidden the jewelry on their bodies. Necklaces were twined lumpily around their legs. Rings, brooches, clasps, and earrings were thrust down into bodices. One young woman held between her knees a sack that contained gold crucifixes, candlesticks, and altar pieces. Selkirk took it from her, and took the rest of the jewelry.

Physical contact with the women sent him back to the night of lust when he had killed the seals and staggered bloodsoaked, screaming along the main beach on the island. But the lack of feeling came to him once more, and he could speak quietly to the sailors. He ordered them not to molest the women and to take the loot to the boat.

He brought the loot back to Guayaquil and gave it to Rogers. It was not at all what they had expected, Rogers said, but there was no more to be had. These Spaniards were a stubborn lot. So the force would leave as soon as the wounded were loaded aboard the boats. There should be better luck in the ships and out to sea, along the coast.

The force rejoined the ships and they shaped a northerly course. For weeks, they lay off Baja California, waiting for the great Manila galleon and her load of gold and silver. The galleon was due on her annual voyage to Acapulco in Mexico.

She arrived, a fine new vessel built of Philippine mahogany and very strongly armed. The English closed at once with their much smaller ships. Then they lowered their boats and made a series of boarding attacks.

The battle lasted for an hour and a half. Selkirk fought the first part of it aboard *Increase*. He rounded her up and set her alongside the Spanish ship. Her name was *Nuestra Señora de la Incarnacion Disenganio*, he found after her master surrendered.

Selkirk had swarmed over the Spanish ship's side holding a cutlass and a pistol, and used both of them. But now the excitement went out of him. He rested slack while the terms of surrender were arranged. He was dreaming of Largo, and of the island. It would not be too long, he knew, before he was home again. He hoped that would make him forget the island.

The little English fleet sailed west from Mexico, the galleon along as a prize. Rogers had been badly wounded in an unsuccessful attack against another Spanish ship, and *Duchess* severely injured. But Rogers laid off a course for Guam, 6,000 miles away.

Guam was reached, and then Ternate in the Moluccas, and Batavia, and the Cape of Good Hope. The battered ships waited in Table Bay for the formation of a Dutch convoy guarded by men-of-war. They left Table Bay with it and in October, 1711, were safe in England. The owners of the expedition made no announcement about the profits from the voyage, but they admitted that the share-out was around a million pounds sterling. Selkirk's payoff was big. He went home proudly to Largo after having been away for more than eight years.

His family was pleased to see him. The expedition was already famous. His brothers who were still at home were friendly, and old feuds were forgotten. Selkirk was not happy, though. The village had become a much different place in his imagination. It was bigger and more beautiful, the way he dreamed it. The drains did not stink, and the fog did not drag in at night from the North Sea, clammy and thick, and fill the narrow streets from wall to wall.

Selkirk went out in the backyard of his father's cottage and dug a cave. He sat in it all day long when it was finished, and gave himself to dreams of the island. He heard the murmur of the island wind, and felt the warmth of the sun, saw the bright and gay little birds unafraid around him, and his pets in play at his feet. The solitude closed gradually but surely, and he was the center of his own universe.

When his mother said that he was a fool and should leave the cave, he did not answer. The neighbors' jokes were meaningless, and after a few weeks they called him the daft hermit, then ignored him. But one of the village girls, Sophia Bonce, came to visit him quite often. She sat down in front of the cave, and unless Selkirk wanted to talk, stayed silent.

Selkirk told her bit by bit about the island, and how he would get back. He would go to Bristol and take a ship bound for the West Indies. Then there was no real trouble to cross the Isthmus of Panama and catch a coasting vessel in the Pacific. The island was only a short sail offshore. A coaster could easily make the run to it from the mainland.

Sophia sat and listened. Then she finally let Selkirk know that she would like to go with him. They left Largo and went to Bristol. Their departure caused talk in the village, because reports from Bristol said that they were living together although unmarried.

Word got back later that Selkirk had been in a fight with a shipwright named Richard Nettle. He was still living with Sophia, and had made out his will in her name. But he suspected that she wanted his money more than anything else. He left Sophia and met a widow, Mrs. Francis Candis.

Mrs. Candis was firm. Selkirk married her at Oarson in Devon, and afterward made out a second will, in her name. She had no intention, though, of going to live on the island. Selkirk went back to sea when he discovered this. He was posted in 1720 as mate in the Royal Navy ship *Weymouth*.

He died the next year while at sea and was buried there. It must have occurred to him during his final service that Captain Stradling had cast him away forever.

The English buccaneers who made a common practice in the seventeenth century of overhauling, boarding, and looting the huge Spanish galleons in the Caribbean had a term of praise for their navigators. They called these men sea-artists. William Dampier was without doubt the finest of the lot. But he was more.

Dampier, who was born a farmer's son in Somersetshire, and who went off to sea in his teens, was a superbly skillful hydrographer, a very good artist, and a writer with a naturally easy, vivid, and pungent style. He wrote about his buccaneer service, "I joined them more to indulge my curiosity than to get wealth." Fact bore him out. The only voyage when he did not come home

*broke was under the command of Captain Woodes Rogers, who
was the sworn and deadly foe of all pirates and buccaneers. It was
on this same voyage that Alexander Selkirk was taken from his
castaway's exile.*

*Curiosity led Dampier to four voyages of circumnavigation.
Half of the oceans were unexplored when he started in the ships.
A great part of Africa was unknown. It was not yet sure whether
Australia was a continent. The coasts of New Guinea and New
Britain had not been touched. Dampier would learn about these;
his implacable curiosity took him to them.*

He left his name on the charts of the world.

WILLIAM DAMPIER

DAMPIER stood knee-deep in water as he swung the
ax. It was double-bladed and heavy, with a long helve.
His hair hung to his shoulders and his beard was thick. This
helped to keep away some of the mosquitoes from his face.
But his body was bare to the waist because of the steamy
jungle heat, and there the mosquitoes and gnats fiercely attacked him.

Still, working on the stubborn trunk of the big logwood
tree, he was happy. He was able to set aside in his thought
the fact that he was alone here in this cove on the Yucatan
coast. A Spanish patrol might emerge any time from the shore
trail, capture him, and send him to Campeche and along to
the Inquisition tortures in High Mexico. His old shipmates

had once said about him that Will Dampier lived a lot more in his head than aboard the vessel.

His presence here was to him wholly logical. He did not ask himself why a man of his intelligence was at work like this, with so little to be made from it. His life, as he looked back, formed an inevitable pattern, right up to the instant that the ax swung in his hands for another stroke.

He was born in the small village of East Coker, near Yeovil, in 1652, the son of William and Joan Dampier, who rented land from the local squire and had another son named George. The boys worked hard alongside their father, but the family made a fair living. Their cottage was well-built and pleasant, called Hymerford House.

The logwood cutter in the Yucatan swamp could distinctly remember it, and the smell of the dooryard lilacs, the cuckoos calling, and the doves. The memories were as clear as the huge, pale orchids here, and the coughing of an alligator in the tidal mud, a jaguar's high, tight scream at night, the chattering of the parrots all day long. The smell of the lilacs returned to him shortly, took the place of the sour, rank jungle decay. Then he lifted and swung the ax.

Each log, when cut, trimmed and hauled to One Bush Cay, where the trading vessels put in, was worth a hundred pounds apiece. If a man sold enough, he could go back wealthy to England, give praise forever that a very popular dye was made from logwood. The usual happening, though, was when the traders came to One Bush Cay they were very liberal with their rum.

The loggers were mostly former soldiers who had served in the British forces on Jamaica. The traders were from Jamaica, brought news, were a source of contact with the outside world. The loggers, after months in the jungle at dawn to dusk labor, became festive, and sentimental, and wildly hilarious. For every drink of rum poured, they insisted that a salute from the vessel's cannon be fired. Before they became senseless and could still sign their marks, they gave away to the traders the sum of their logwood haul for rum, shot and powder, and a small amount of flour and tobacco.

One Bush Cay was named for the solitary cabbage palm that grew on the small, sandy island. The morning after a trader had left on his way back to Jamaica it was filled with deeply drunken loggers. They slept until the Yucatan sun penetrated the rum fog. Some were sick; others had enough strength to take a dip in the sea and think about food. The group gradually gathered sense, and counted the few shillings worth of goods left them by the trader.

But they were philosophical about the fact that the trader had sorely cheated them. The freedom from outside influences, the almost primeval quality of their existence, held an enormous appeal for them. They were not outlaws. They had come here of their own will and in reality paid a very great deal for the freedom they found.

Logwood trees grew only in swampy land where working conditions were invariably miserable. The men were threatened by alligators and snakes in the swamps, and by jaguars and Spanish patrols on solid ground. Their swollen, battered feet were constantly infected by chiggers. Malaria, dysentery, and gangrene were common and often fatal among them. They called their sleeping shelters "pavilions," but these were no more than sailcloth tents closely secured to keep out mosquitoes.

Dampier came to the Yucatan coast in February, 1676, from Jamaica, and stayed nearly three years. He had previously served as an enlisted man in the Royal Navy during the war against the Dutch, and before that sailed in English merchant ships. He wrote about himself, "My friends did not originally design me for the sea, but bred me at school till I came to years fit for a trade. But upon the death of my father and mother, they who had disposal of me took other measures; and having remov'd me from the Latine Schoole to learn Writing and Arithmetick, they soon after placed me with a Master of a Ship at Weymouth, complying with the inclinations I had very early of seeing the world."

Dampier went out to the West Indies in 1674 to work as the manager of a sugar plantation. He was twenty-two and a hard-bitten young veteran, discharged from the Royal Navy because of illness. The plantation was owned by the local squire at home, Colonel Helyer, from whom his father had rented land as a tenant farmer. But Dampier did not like the Jamaican life where several hundred Negro slaves and white indentured people were driven daily in the fields under the lash.

A coaster captain needed an experienced hand on the Yucatan run. Dampier sailed with him, and when the ship came to the One Bush Cay anchorage, left her. He started the next day as a logwood-cutter.

A hurricane ended the logwood trade in June, 1678. It smashed and tangled the coastal forest so that further work was impossible. The storm struck with vicious, enormous force, and very early in the usual hurricane season. Dampier had already formed the habit of keeping a journal; he recorded in it many of the storm details which later were to become part of his famous *Discourse on the Trade Winds*.

He and the other loggers who were still alive after the first terrific gusts had wrenched through the forest, toppling tree upon tree and whipping inland a twenty-foot tide, survived at Terminos Lagoon. They lay flat beneath fallen trees and listened to the scream, the shriek, the whine of the storm, and the crash of the awful surf, the grind of torn branches, the thrash of spindrift that was so hard-driven it cut like a knife, and all the small, confused, and multiple sounds made by leaves and lianas and bushes and plants as the wind destroyed them.

Then the wind swung. The rain stopped, and the sun came forth red and very bright.

The loggers knew that the hurricane would return from the opposite direction, but now they had a couple of free hours. They moved to higher, safer ground and did what they could for the men who had been trapped under trees. Dampier took his journal out of the waterproof sailcloth covering, sharpened his quill, opened his precious ink, and hastily but neatly wrote the storm account. He added to that later when the second phase of the hurricane was completed. His companions had started a fire and were cooking some of the more edible fish taken from the beach. He joined them and they talked of very practical matters.

The destruction here meant the logwood trade was finished. They had been poor men before; now they had no living of any sort. But, one of them said, they still had their cutlasses and muskets and a few pistols. They were nearly all veterans, and knew where to find the Spaniards who had raided them many times.

Dampier fully understood the talk. A raid, an act of piracy was being planned. It would very likely lead to others. Some of these men were already called buccaneers by their companions. They had been "on the account," served in ships that attacked Spanish settlements in Cuba and Hispaniola.

Dampier voted for the raid. He moved out with the rest of the men when the hurricane had spent itself. They marched along the coast until they reached the town of Alvarado, near Vera Cruz. The place had a strong garrison, and the Spaniards had been warned of their coming. The fight was hard, sharp.

But the Englishmen took the town and thoroughly looted it. Dampier wrote in his journal that his share was "a few pounds." He bought his passage home to England with the money, sailed from Jamaica. He had been away for four and a half years when he arrived in August, 1678, and had only the journal to show his brother George in East Coker.

He tried to control the great desire to go to sea, "the curiosity" about the world which was to dominate his life. He met and married in that same year of his homecoming a woman named Judith. There is no more known about her except that she came from "the household of the Duke of Grafton." She and Dampier were together until the spring of 1679, and then he left again for Jamaica.

The urge to go back to sea was too strong. And he chose to serve in the Caribbean as a buccaneer. The buccaneer life held many attractions for Englishmen, Scots, Irish, Dutch, and French.

Life at home was extremely difficult for them in their countries. Wealth was held by the very few. Poverty was widespread, and there was no middle class. Crime was punished with the utmost, brutal severity, and any healthy young man was seized for long and practically payless military service. To turn buccaneer if the chance afforded was about the only solution left.

A powerful buccaneer force of several hundred men and a number of ships was outfitting at Negril Bay when Dampier reached Jamaica. He instantly joined it. The leaders, veteran buccaneer captains, were planning the sack of the rich Spanish town of Puerto Bello on the Caribbean side of the Isthmus of Panama.

The raid was successful, the town taken without much

loss of life, and a considerable amount of loot collected. The leaders decided to continue the expedition, and the force went south to Darien, started across after the ships were careened and camouflaged in the backwaters of a cove.

The traverse from the Caribbean coast began April 5, 1680, and the buccaneers were pleased that most of it was made in Cimaroon dugout canoes along the rivers that threaded the isthmus. The Cimaroons were local people, a mixture of indigenous Indians and runaway Negro slaves. They hated the Spaniards for their cruelty and were pleased to serve the Englishmen as guides.

The immediate objective was the stockaded Spanish town of Santa Maria. It was more fort than town and around it the Spaniards worked poorly paying, surface gold mines with slave labor. A famous Cimaroon chieftain, a man the buccaneers called King Golden Cap, joined their column outside the town. Golden Cap's daughter had been captured by the Spaniards and was a prisoner here. He showed the buccaneers the way into the stockade, went with the first of them.

This was at night. Men fought in darkness, then by torchlight and the blaze of burning buildings. Two buccaneers were killed in the assault, and two Cimaroon warriors, and forty Spaniards. There were 220 men of the garrison left alive when the commander surrendered. The Cimaroons killed all of them.

Dampier, cutlass in hand, watched the slaughter. He made a careful record of it later in his journal. His description of the horror was factual. What the Spaniards had done to the slaves and to King Golden Cap's daughter very probably dulled his senses.

The loot was small at Santa Maria. When the Englishmen reached the Pacific Coast close to the Bay of Panama they were very eager for combat. The captains of the various buccaneer companies took them to it in Cimaroon canoes. They boarded several big Spanish ships in full daylight, and with the cutlass and the pistol butt against cannon, seized two of them.

But in this action the buccaneers heavily paid. They lost eighteen men killed and twenty-two wounded. Dampier wrote in the journal that the Spaniards lost many more. Then he and the rest of the force made a swiftly executed raid upon Puebla Nueva, at the mouth of a mainland river.

Captain Sawkins led the attack up from the beach and was almost instantly killed. Many of the men around him were killed right afterward by the sharp Spanish fire. But the next group of buccaneers sprinted past the dead, climbed the gun embrasures, and got among the Spaniards with the cutlass. Then surrender came.

Puebla Nueva was captured May 25, 1680, and at the shareout of the loot the men decided that they still had time to raid along the coast. But there was a lot of quarreling after several more raids had been made. Some men were afraid of capture and being subjected to the Inquisition in Lima. Most of the others had gambled away their shares of loot and saw no reason to fight any further.

Dampier and forty-four other men made the choice to leave the expedition. It was time to start up the coast, cross over to Darien and get clear away from the Spaniards. They had their muskets, their cutlasses and pistols, a little powder, shot, and food. Darien and Golden Island Cove, where their original ship was hidden, were 500 miles away.

Dampier wrote about the journey, part of which was made northward along the coast in canoes, and the rest overland through thick jungle:

"And because there were some who designed to go with us that we knew were not well able to march, we gave out that if any Man faltered in the Journey over Land he must expect to be shot to Death; for we knew that the Spaniards would soon be after us, and one man falling into their hands might be the ruin of us all, by giving an account of our Strength and Condition."

The group kept to their canoes until they were warned by friendly people ashore that a big Spanish ship was approaching from the northward. They left the coast and began the dreaded overland march that would take weeks of unbroken effort.

The men were barefoot, half-starved, sick with fever, dysentery, infected feet. They came hobbling to a deep and rapid river which could not be forded and must be swum. Men threw away their muskets and their cutlasses. They tossed into the bamboo brakes their sacks of Spanish loot. Then they eased down into the water and swam.

Dampier waited until he was the last. Then he picked a sturdy bamboo and cut it carefully with his cutlass. He rolled his journal tight and put it inside the piece of bamboo. He sealed the ends with tapered parts taken from the same section of bamboo and jammed hard to make them waterproof.

Dampier swam the river and all of the other rivers on the way to Darien with his journal intact. He was going to take it to London and get it printed. This was his loot.

The march lasted twenty days, and during it two of the buccaneers and the party's affable, efficient surgeon, Lionel Wafer, were forced to drop out because of their weakened condition. But their companions did not shoot them, and eventually they also reached the Caribbean coast, aided by the Cimaroons. The Cimaroons were of great help to the buccaneers. They hunted wild turkeys and monkeys in the jungle for meat, and acted as guides along the entire 110-mile route from the Pacific.

When the party came out at Golden Island Cove, a French privateer ship was anchored close inshore. The buccaneers felt immense relief; they would be safe from the Spaniards with the French ship here. They went aboard her and bought all the beads, mirrors, and other small trade goods the Frenchmen carried. The presents only cost a couple of shillings a man, Dampier reported, but they delighted the Cimaroons.

Golden Island had become a well-known buccaneer rendezvous, and the lot that had arrived from the Pacific were soon offered further service. They joined an English ship and went to the southward in her and raided several Spanish settlements. Then Dampier and some of the other men decided that they should give up "the account" for a while. They had enough loot to rest easy, and took passage for Virginia.

Dampier enjoyed peace and legality for a full year. He went back to the buccaneer trade when Captain John Cook entered the Chesapeake aboard a fine, recently captured French ship. The captain was looking for recruits, and proposed to sail around Cape Horn and enter the Pacific, raid the Spaniards from Payta to Panama. There was no hesitation on Dampier's part; he signed to sail with Cook.

Captain Cook called the ship *Revenge*. She carried eighteen guns and a full crew of 70 men. Dampier was assigned as assistant quartermaster. This meant he was the navigator and, in buccaneer terms of rank, he was third in command aboard. His direct superior was a famous buccaneer named Edward Davis. Davis served as chief quartermaster and was capable of taking over the ship at any time from Cook.

Dampier, once the ship was at sea, kept his journal and made a record of all that happened. His quarters were a bit better, now he was assistant quartermaster, and he could work at night, using a lantern without waking up men who stretched in their hammocks close around him. He rigged a canvas screen between his sleeping space and the crew's quarters, wrote or drew sketches and diagrams until it was time to go on watch.

Revenge rounded Cape Horn in good style and stood northward to Juan Fernandez Island. She was accompanied by a ship they had captured in the Atlantic and named *Batchelor's Delight*. The buccaneer ships stayed for sixteen days and then went up the coast to raid.

It was the familiar story of the plunder of the Spanish towns, but without much success. Payta was raided, and Puna, and Puebla Nueva. The buccaneers stayed away from Panama, though, and considered it too tough to take.

There was dissension among the buccaneers. Crews voted, and captains lost command. Dampier chose to go aboard an English buccaneer ship named *Cygnet* that had been operating alone for some time on the coast. *Cygnet* was commanded by Captain Swan, who had a great reputation as a buccaneer master, and who talked of sailing into the far reaches of the Pacific. This fascinated Dampier, and took him aboard *Cygnet*.

She sailed from off the Mexican coast on March 31, 1686, and started across the Pacific for the Ladrone Islands. It was a voyage of almost incredible daring. Neither Captain Swan nor Dampier, who served as his navigator, was at all sure of the exact position of the landfall. They knew that their longitude reckoning, because of the lack of correct charts and mathematical tables and a reliable timepiece, must be partly approximation.

Their food was limited to a half-pint of coarse Indian corn a man a day. The voyage lasted 52 days. When landfall was made on the Ladrones there was a supply of three days' rations left. But Dampier had been able to get many fine observations of the sun. He brought *Cygnet* in right on course.

The crew, once the anchor was down and the men had stretched their legs ashore, became mutinous. They wanted to know just how Swan proposed to make their fortunes for them in this part of the world. Swan was accustomed to the talk. He told the men not to get worried. They would seize the Manila galleon on her annual voyage eastward to Mexico. She carried each voyage a vast amount of wealth, mainly in gold bullion, gathered in the Philippines and consigned to Spain as the king's property. Any man of *Cygnet's* crew who failed to be patient and wait for that prize, Swan said, was so stupid that he should be keel-hauled by his shipmates.

Dampier listened to Swan along with the rest and kept quiet. But he was not satisfied with what the captain said. He knew as a navigator that in the enormous spaces of this ocean it was practically impossible for *Cygnet* to intercept the galleon. And she was the only prize they could hope to capture. There were no more like her in the Pacific. This was not the Caribbean where there was constant ship movement, or even the west coast of South America with Spanish trading vessels and the port towns to be looted.

Cygnet, cranky to the helm, her bottom foul and her sails rotted by sea damp and sun exposure, sailed a number of intercept courses for the galleon. She missed the Spanish ship although she ranged from Guam to Mindanao to the Nicobar Islands. The basic discipline needed for a successful voyage was missing, and the crew spent six months ashore in Mindanao, with *Cygnet* at anchor offshore. Then they took her back to sea. But there was bad feeling among them. Fights started, and Captain Swan and thirty-six men were put ashore. Dampier stayed with the remainder. He wrote in his journal that he was tired of "this roving life." There was no reason why the entire ship's company shouldn't settle down ashore. The men aboard *Cygnet* had among them carpenters, bricklayers, shoemakers, and tailors. They could establish in the soft and warm, plentiful climate of these islands a society which, because of their European skills, they could easily dominate. But each of them wanted to be free from any restraint, and would accept no responsibility that reached beyond tomorrow.

Dampier realized that existence aboard *Cygnet* could only end in disaster. He asked to be put ashore at one of the smaller Nicobar islands with his gear, and the buccaneer council that ran the ship let him go. A few other men, also worried by what was ahead, went along, and made him their leader.

The island was wild jungle beyond the beach. It offered them nothing; they could not stay here. Dampier understood their danger. *Cygnet* was gone, and would not return. They had cast themselves away in one of the most desolate, uncivilized areas in the world. If they wanted to survive, they must get out right away.

Dampier talked with his companions. They agreed to his plan to try to reach the English factory at Achin, on the island of Sumatra, 150 miles to the westward across open sea. But he knew that only one of them, a man named Robert Hall, had any recognition of the danger they must meet during the voyage. They exchanged an ax for a Malay dugout canoe and shoved off for Sumatra.

The craft had exactly, according to Dampier's careful calculations, a three-inch freeboard. He intended to sail and paddle her on the traverse where sharks were a constant menace and gales were frequent. This was the low point of his life. He could never be any more desperate than when he waded out into the surf, stowed his belongings, climbed aboard the canoe, and took up the steering paddle.

Seven men were in the party, all of them buccaneers and greatly experienced at handling small craft in surf. But they were unable to do much with the dugout. She took a wave aboard while still in the surf, filled and capsized. The men swam her back to the beach and got the water out of her, but Dampier did not make another try.

He talked in sign language with the Malay fisherman who had sold them the canoe. The man was willing, for a small present, to equip her with an outrigger and to restep the mast that carried a mat sail. The flotation factor was considerably improved. When the next try was made in the surf, it was successful. Dampier squatted down in the sternsheets, took a firm grip on the paddle and the sail sheet, set his course for Sumatra.

He realized once more when offshore how great the risk was. Still, the voyage was by no means hopeless. He had studied with the utmost care the East Indies chart before he left *Cygnet*, and entered a number of pilotage directions in his pocket notebook. He also had a pocket compass, kept it between his knees as he steered.

Gales hit them hard during the two-day voyage. Dampier lowered the sail and ran the canoe before the wind while the men desperately bailed with their hands, coconut shells, and their raffia hats. She rode the weather, climbed each wave, and when the last heavy wind passed, Dampier came back to course for Sumatra. The island rose from the sea jade green and amethyst and purple under cloud shadow.

The cloud was still wracked by storm, and whipped into long, thin banners of dark yellow.

The men could smell the spice trees and, with a shift in the wind, hear a tiger roar in the jungle. They talked excitedly about what they would do here, and the help they were sure to get from the English at Achin. But Dampier was counting the hours since they had left the island in the Nicobar group, and figuring how he would head the canoe through the surf.

He saw the palm thatch roofs and the beached canoes of a small fishing village, brought the canoe around and pointed her directly inshore. The fishermen were silent when the men beached the canoe and dragged her past the surf line. They gave no gesture of greeting, simply stood aside when the buccaneers staggered into the village.

The voyage had been short, but the results of it were severe. Dampier and the others had been sitting in cramped postures for more than forty-eight hours, their feet and legs immersed in sea water. They suffered from sea boils, cramp, and hunger. Now they walked with immense difficulty.

There was an empty hut at the edge of the village. Dampier led the men into it. They sprawled out side by side on old raffia mats where rats had nested. They slept, then drifted off into the early stages of malaria.

They lay in the hut for two weeks while, day and night, the dapper little Malays stood wordless in the doorway and stared at them. The village where they had landed was about 100 miles from Achin, and there was nobody here who would give them help. But Dampier finally got back a bit of his strength.

He went from the hut and found fresh fruit and drinking water. Then he opened up his sea chest, lugged along the beach from the canoe. He dried the pages of his journal in the sun. They were still legible, and he was immensely pleased. He smoothed the pages and put them in order and made an entry below that which marked the May 15, 1688, departure from Nicobar.

"I had long before this repented me of that roving Course of Life, but never with such concern as now."

He left the fishing village with his shipmates and solemnly told himself he was going back to England just as soon as he could get there. He navigated the dugout coastwise and brought her to Achin with all hands in pretty fair health. The English people at the trading factory were glad to help them, and the castaways were assured of passage home.

But wanderlust was a very deep part of Dampier's nature. He saw no reason to go home when he might wander around the Orient for a while and maybe make his fortune. He and his buccaneer shipmate, Robert Hall, who had proven himself an excellent sailor in the dugout, were approached at Achin by an English captain named Weldon.

Weldon was owner and master of a China Seas trading vessel. He recruited Dampier and Hall to make a voyage with him to Tonkin. It was a very pleasant experience after what they had just gone through, and the two reformed buccaneers enjoyed all of it. Dampier had fallen in love with the Orient. He was excited by the busy, noisy, always colorful ports, the praus, the junks, the sampans, the harbor shouts, the temple bells, the gongs, the cymbals, and the people who were so active and so gay, and indolent. He almost forgot about England and why he should return there.

He had been offered command of a trading schooner by Weldon, and accepted, sailed in her on a voyage to the Cochin China coast. But the malaria that had afflicted him since he was in Sumatra kept him in the bunk most of the time, and along with that he suffered from dysentery. His mate handled the ship. All Dampier could do was sit up on deck and make notes in his journal and sketches of the coast.

When he got his health back, he served as mate in various vessels trading in the North and the South China Seas and among the great island chains and archipelagos to the eastward. But he ended up nearly broke in the port of Bencoolen, on the southwest coast of Sumatra. Some of the Oriental glamor had become tarnished for him, and he felt a poignant need to return to England. Then his constantly active mind was attracted by a waterfront figure he had first seen on exhibit in Mindanao.

This was a battered and bemused but still amazingly robust Melanesian warrior known either as "Prince Jeoly" or "The Painted Prince." The man was tall, his skin blue-black, and his hair a kinky mass that sprouted high upward from his skull. He was tattooed from his brows to his ankles, front and back, in exotic pictograph designs. He had been captured in some tribal canoe raid on a Pacific atoll, been shipped around for sale and resale ever since. His present owner was an Englishman named Moody, and impressed by the need for cash at home, Dampier bought a half-interest in the Prince.

There was after that a tense wait for a ship that was bound for England. It had been Dampier's good luck to interest the local governor with his accomplishments, and he had been given personal quarters in Bencoolen Fort. His understanding with the governor, though, was to stay for a considerable period of time, serve as instructor for a course in navigation and coastal survey. When the English ship *Defence* came into port and her master, Captain Heath, said he was London-bound, Dampier went to the governor. He asked permission to sail. It was flatly refused.

Dampier talked privately with Prince Jeoly. He impressed upon the Prince the need for secrecy if they were to get to London together and make their fortunes. Midnight of the night before *Defence* sailed, Dampier slipped the Prince through a gun embrasure of Bencoolen Fort. He led the Prince down to the beach and a boat from the ship, and they embarked. But Dampier had left behind him his navigation instruments, his charts, his books and drafts, his clothes and bedding, even his small supply of money, everything except his journal. It was the only way he could outwit the governor's guards and escape.

Defence sailed from Bencoolen on January 2, 1691, and made a miserable passage. She arrived off The Downs on September 18 with half her crew dead because of fever, scurvy, and dysentery. Dampier landed with the Prince and went to London. He had been gone for twelve years, came back absolutely penniless.

He put Prince Jeoly up for public display in London just as soon as he could arrange to get the use of a hall on credit. Jeoly drew a reasonably large crowd of the curious, and Dampier, with a couple of guineas in his pocket, made an investment in a handbill that was distributed throughout the city and described his prize. It read:

"The Pictures and those other engraven Figures painted from him, and now dispersed abroad, serve only to describe as much as they can of the Fore-parts of this inimitable Piece of workmanship. The more admirable Back Parts afford us a Lively Representation of one quarter part of the World upon and betwixt his shoulders, where the Arcktick and Tropick Circles center in the North Pole on his Neck."

Dampier was able to sell the Prince after this short but intensive advertising campaign. The new owner took Jeoly on a tour of England, and was successful until he exhibited him in Oxford. The penetrant winter cold had gradually worn away the Prince's strength. He was forced because of the nature of the display to appear for hours at a time almost completely naked. He was already badly debilitated by exposure when he contracted smallpox in Oxford and died in a sidestreet tavern room.

Dampier had gone on home to Somerset and found his wife, Judith. He was reunited with her and with his brother when news came of Prince Jeoly's death. Dampier, once more immersed in the beatitude of the English countryside, must have sat solitary for quite some time as he contemplated the life and death of the Prince. He went back in his mind to the far atolls from which Jeoly came.

The palms that ringed the gray-black coral were bent perpetually to the Trade Wind. Spindrift jumped as high as the palm fronds when a big roller came inshore, and the men tossing their nets out on the barrier reef were careful where they crouched across the canoe outriggers. Shark patrolled back and forth right below the surface. But, inside the lagoon, it was calm, and safe. The little children happily splashed and dived. The women, where they sat and pounded taro root, sang with the wind blowing softly in their hair.

Dampier started to write soon after he was at home with Judith. His brother supported him, and then he made money from his writing. He worked long hours daily at the journal he had carried across the rivers on the jungle march to Golden Island, saved from the sea in Nicobar, and sneaked out of Bencoolen Fort past the Malay guards. Now he felt his power. Now the past made sense, and the future, and he went to London with the completed book and found a publisher.

The book was called *Voyage Around the World*. His publisher was James Knapton. It appeared in 1697 and was an instantaneous success. William Dampier, the farmer's son, the logwood-cutter and buccaneer and China Seas drifter, was famous. He had dedicated the book to Charles Montague, the President of the Royal Society, and soon met through Montague some of England's leading intellectuals. He became friendly with Sir Robert Southwell, President of the Royal Society from 1690 to 1695, and Sir Hans Sloane, an internationally known diplomat and patron of the arts and sciences. Sir Hans had been Secretary of the Royal Society in 1693 and maintained a close relationship with Sir Isaac Newton.

With all these men, Dampier was simple, unaffected. They were able to grasp at once that he did not seek much for himself beyond acceptance of his work. He was asked to dine at Samuel Pepys' house with Charles Evelyn, who held a great reputation as a literary figure and a numismatist. Evelyn wrote later of Dampier that he was remarkably unassuming and much more eager to listen than to talk.

Arrangements were made to publish Dampier's other work, his *Supplement* to *Voyage Round the World*, and an account of his logwood-cutter days, *Voyage to Campeachy*, and the book whose source material he had cherished all along, *Discourse on the Trade Winds*.

His portrait was commissioned and painted by Thomas Murray, then hung in the National Portrait Gallery. It showed him as a man of rather slender build and middle height, his dark brown hair long about his strong-boned face. His eyes shone blue, bright against the skin made ruddy by years of tropical sun and sea wind. The nose was beaked and powerful; the chin round, firm.

The artist had obviously been very much attracted by the extraordinary qualities of the sitter. Murray discovered in Dampier's expression some of the strangely brooding intensity, and the almost tragic look of hurt held by the wide-set eyes. Dampier rested remote, drawn backward from the world into some obscure, confused region of loneliness where he lived solitary and in pain. The inscription at the bottom of the picture frame said plainly, *William Dampier, Pirate and Hydrographer.*

Dampier was at home for five years before he told Judith that he was about to return to sea. There was nothing that she could say, and she had already been given warning. During the shore years, and particularly along toward the last of them, when his books were finished, he had shipped out several times as mate in North Sea vessels.

Now, though, he proposed a really long voyage, a circumnavigation. His fame had brought him command of a Royal Navy ship, and he took her to sea in January, 1699, before the rest of his books were published. But he knew right after he boarded her that she was unseaworthy, would offer great trouble. She was HMS *Roebuck*, a fifth-rate frigate that mounted twelve guns and carried a crew of fifty men and boys. The last survey had condemned her to service as a fire-ship, but Admiralty order saved her from that and turned her over to Dampier for exploration purposes.

Disaster rode with Dampier during that voyage. He was not prepared for command, and certainly not for command in a Royal Navy ship. His modest, quiet nature, and the long years in the buccaneer ships were against it. He had always served in a subordinate capacity at sea except for the one brief China Sea voyage. Buccaneer discipline had been a matter of popular vote. Here, in His Majesty's Ship *Roebuck*, it was enforced with the lash, being triced up by the thumbs in the rigging, or placed in irons.

Dampier, one of the finest navigators to ever take a ship to sea, proved almost immediately to be a poor and indecisive captain. He had under him as his executive officer a man who was excessively jealous of Dampier's appointment to command and determined to take it from him. This was a hulking Irishman named George Fisher, who had served in the army before joining the navy.

He held the rank of lieutenant, looked upon himself as a consummate professional officer. Fisher was quick to criticize Dampier in the wardroom and on deck before the junior officers, and then was bold enough to taunt him about his buccaneer past. He intimated, broadly, that Dampier was going to seize the ship for piratical use.

Dampier let Fisher be for some weeks. He took the ship into the Cape Verde Islands for water and provisions, then headed her for Brazil. He kept to himself as much as possible, feeling alien in this world of orders, regulations, strictly observed customs, and unremitting regard for seniority, rank, and grade. But Fisher was unduly brutal with one of the midshipmen, beat the youth until he could hardly stand upright. Then, as *Roebuck* crossed the Equator, Fisher gave his personal order to the cook to broach a cask of beer in celebration of the fact.

That finished Dampier's patience. He reverted to buccaneer tactics, and beat Fisher worse than Fisher had beaten the midshipman. He chased the bigger, stronger man along the deck and into his cabin and locked him there. When Fisher was sure that Dampier had spent his rage, he yelled out the porthole that the crew should take care—the captain was ready to turn pirate and seize the ship.

Dampier let Fisher yell himself speechless. He kept the lieutenant in the small and hot cabin for days without any sanitary facilities. Fisher was a very subdued man when the ship raised the Brazilian coast and Dampier sailed her into Bahia.

Dampier wanted him out of the ship, put him ashore at once in Bahia. This was a mistake for which Dampier was to pay dearly later, because Fisher was the stubborn kind of troublemaker. The lieutenant, as soon as he returned to England, made a lengthy report to the Admiralty and brought charges against Dampier that could only be resolved by court-martial.

But Dampier's great interest was exploration. He nursed the wallowing, leaky, and sluggish *Roebuck* around Cape Horn and then across the Pacific. One of his major purposes was to discover all he could about Australia, and he made his landfall there, sent boat parties ashore at frequent intervals along the western coast. They needed an armed guard to protect them while they looked for fresh water. The wiry, naked natives were fiercely unfriendly, and it was impossible to get any distance from the beach.

Dampier went ashore himself. He found nothing but desert, kangaroo rats, and the boomerang-hurling natives. He took *Roebuck* off the Australian coast in September and shaped a course for Timor. She was in extremely bad condition, with her pumps constantly at work, and at Fort Concordia he careened and repaired her.

Then he ran for New Guinea and explored the wild and mountainous south coast. He held *Roebuck* carefully offshore from the great, bunched coral heads while he made his geodetic notations and contour sketches, afterward hauled around on a Northwest course. He had taken his New Guinea landfall January 1, 1700, and now he rounded the northernmost part of the vast, continent-like island. He held to the southward after that, coasting, slowly entering the strait between New Guinea and New Britain Island.

The weather was fitful, with many heavy squalls. The ship was leaking badly again, and every breeze off the land brought mosquitoes in khaki-colored hordes from the rain forest. Dampier decided that he had done enough exploration for His Majesty. He put the ship on a course for Ceram, where he hoped that he could further repair her.

The crew did all that they could for *Roebuck* at Ceram, and Dampier told the men that now they were homeward-bound. They cleared the Cape of Good Hope on December 30 and on February 2, 1701, they were abreast of St. Helena. It was the end of the haul. *Roebuck* was finished. Dampier wrote in his journal, "We sprung a leak which increased so that the chain pump could not keep the ship free."

He worked her toward the shore with his anchors out ahead, in a kedging operation. Water poured into her, slopped from the lower holds into the tween decks. She listed, and began to sink in three fathoms. There was no more time.

The carpenter had been making a raft out of spare spars and gratings. The cook put a supply of fresh water and rice aboard it, and the men hurried to bring their sea chests from the fo'c'sle. But Dampier, who took command of the launching of the raft, lost many of his books and papers. He had stayed on deck too long, could not now go below to his cabin.

The raft reached the black sand beach propelled by oars and the men's hands. Dampier landed and looked around and knew that they would not starve. This was much easier than his last landing as a castaway. He had just seen turtles as they scampered behind the rocks along the beach. Turtle meat and turtle eggs, he remembered from his Caribbean days, made a good diet.

Dampier was on St. Helena for five weeks with his crew. Then four English ships touched the island in the regular fashion homeward-bound from the Cape of Good Hope. They were after fresh water, firewood, and possibly a turtle, were willing to accommodate the castaways. Dampier went home April 3, 1701, in the ship *Canterbury*, as he noted in the journal, "accompanied with my Master, Purser, Gunner, and three of my superior officers."

He was called before a court-martial right after his return to England and forced to defend himself against charges brought by his former lieutenant. Fisher had friends in the Admiralty, and there were a number of Royal Navy officers who held no liking for a man with a record of service as a buccaneer. Dampier was found guilty. The court-martial's decision was that he had mistreated Fisher. This meant disgrace, and he was no longer the popular figure asked out to dinner by the London intellectuals.

He left London, relieved of all Royal Navy duty, and went to Somersetshire to live with Judith. He was not allowed much time there, though. The War of the Spanish succession had begun, and England fought against both Spain and France. Veteran officers were needed, and Prince George of Denmark, the Lord High Admiral, called upon Dampier to take command of a privateer.

Dampier wrote in his journal about his return to grace: "Being prepared to depart on another voyage to the West Indies, had the honour to kiss Her Majesty's hand, being introduced by His Royal Highness, the Lord High Admiral."

The old buccaneer was ready to accept a bit of flattering attention from royalty. Privateers were an important part of the war at sea, and he understood the fact. He was given a good, well-supplied ship and issued a privateer commission. It made any future acts of depredation at sea legal under English law—if not under Spanish or French.

His ship was named *St. George.* She mounted twenty-six guns, and the Admiralty had allowed him 120 men for a crew. He took her to sea on April 30, 1703 and, according to orders, went to anchor May 18 off the Irish coast. The *Cinque Ports,* a 50-ton galley also serving as an English privateer, kept rendezvous with Dampier's vessel there. The two ships sailed in company for Cape Horn.

They were headed for the famous buccaneer raiding grounds along the West Coast of South America instead of the West Indies. But a storm separated them near Cape Horn. When Dampier reached Juan Fernandez toward the last of February, *Cinque Ports* had already been at anchor off the island for three weeks.

There was bitter dissension in the *Cinque Ports* crew. Thomas Stradling, who had recently become her captain, was a tough disciplinarian. He sent his sailing master, a man named Alexander Selkirk, ashore and left him there, and then sailed off after Spanish loot.

Dampier was perplexed. He did a little raiding on the coast, but there were too many Spanish patrol ships guarding the ports. It would be better, he decided, to make the Pacific traverse and try to seize the Manila galleon on her way east from the Philippines.

He allowed himself to forget the grim failure of *Cygnet's* last voyage. Disaster came to him again in this ship. The crew, hungry, weary, turned mutinous when *St. George* reached Timor. The privateer commission that had been issued to Dampier in London was no longer effective. The Dutch officials looked upon him as a pirate and threatened him with arrest if he didn't get out of their colonial waters.

Dampier gave up command of the ship. He left her and the crew in Timor and returned home alone, broke, and as a workaway. It was his third voyage of circumnavigation and a total failure.

He found when he got back to England that both his wife and his brother were dead. There was a cousin, a middle-aged woman named Grace Mercer, who lived in London, and he went to stay with her. But he was still strong and active and greatly loved the sea. When Captain Woodes Rogers of Dover asked him to join a new privateer expedition as chief pilot, he said that he would be very glad to sail.

Dampier sailed in *Duke* with Captain Rogers and the noisy Doctor Dover. He made the famous voyage of circumnavigation during which Selkirk was taken from Juan Fernandez and then the Manila galleon was seized. His share of the Spanish loot was handsome. It was paid by the backers of the expedition in October, 1711, after *Duke* returned to England.

He made his home again with his cousin in London. He died there on March 1, 1715. Forty-two years of his life had been spent at sea.

There was quiet here at the entrance of the Mexican river during the sun-hard afternoon. The waves of the great gulf moved easily among the mangrove roots on the beach; turtles sidled from the mud; and once and again a macaw called. For the boys and the men aboard Minion, the lack of sound was painful. They had come from battle and from weeks of hurricane. They stood strained, pale, and sweaty in front of John Hawkins on the shattered main deck.

Hawkins had led them in the battle at San Juan de Ulua on September 17, 1567, fourteen days before. He had taken command of Minion and sailed her free from the Spaniards in the narrow harbor where the English had been trapped on the east coast of Mexico. Now he mustered the company that counted two hundred, and he was bitterly aware that he could not bring all of them back with him to England.

Minion had suffered enormous damage in the pair of hurricanes that had struck her and the other two English ships off the western end of Cuba. Then the Spanish gunners at San Juan de Ulua served her with point-blank salvos. Her seams gaped. Her upper works were sprung and a shambles. Water gurgled unchecked into her hold while Hawkins stood and chose the words he must pronounce.

It was going to be a near-starvation passage home. Rats, cats, and the crew's pet parrots and dogs had already been eaten. So part of the company would have to leave the ship here, risk capture by the Spaniards.

Hawkins spoke straight. He told those who wished to go ashore to step forward of the foremast; those who wished to sail should stand abaft it. Ninety-six of the company were willing to try the shore instead of the passage home in unseaworthy Minion on short rations during the North Atlantic winter gales.

He gave six yards of trade cloth to each man who wished to stay. Some said they should have money, and Hawkins supplied them with it. Then he embraced all of them separately and looked intently into their faces. He promised them that if God sent him safely home, he would do what he could to bring the lot back to England.

The ninety-six went ashore from Minion *after that. The pinnace that had carried them returned to the ship. The anchor was brought short as sail was bent to the light breeze.* Minion *came about and headed into the immense sun dazzle over the Gulf of Mexico. She was clumsy, sluggish to the helm, and dangerously low in the water.*

A number of the younger boys wept, though, as she went behind the horizon curve, the sun bright on her baggy topsails. She meant home. With her gone, hope disappeared.

Job Hortop stood among the company on the beach. He had been Captain Hawkins' gunner. He was a veteran and recognized his responsibility as a chief petty officer. The company should go inland at once, he said. There was nothing to do them any good here along the sea.

JOB HORTOP

THEY WALKED through the jungle close to the river while the daylight lasted. Hortop and some of the others knew that the river was named Panuco and led to a town of the same name,* but that was all. They camped with darkness and made a fire and sat knee to knee. Fear of tomorrow kept them awake, and hunger.

It was inevitable that they should talk about the battle. Hortop half-listened, saying nothing, conjecturing out of his experience what might happen to them at the hands of the Indians or the Spaniards. Here in this region, he knew, the

---

* Present-day Tampico.

Indians were allies of the Spaniards, worked submissively, and took their orders from the nearest garrison commander.

If the Indians caught them and let them live, Hortop told himself, then the company would very probably be turned over to the Spaniards at the town of Panuco. That was the start of the slavery road up into High Mexico, and probably lifelong imprisonment. A lot of Spaniards had been killed in the battle at San Juan de Ulua. The Viceroy at Mexico City wouldn't feel much sympathy for English prisoners.

Hortop withdrew his thought from contemplation of the future. It was too grim. He joined in discussion of the battle details being retold again in the jungle-noisy night.

There had been three English ships engaged, *Jesus of Lubeck*, which was John Hawkins' original command, and *Minion*, and *Judith*, commanded by Hawkins' cousin, Francis Drake. The cousins had left England in 1567 with great expectations of loot to be taken on the Spanish Main with small loss to them. But they were wrong.

The officers of the garrisons in the various ports along the Main, remembering past English raids, were prepared to defend themselves. The Spaniards fought shrewdly, and if forced to evacuate a town, took with them or quite successfully hid anything of value. The pickings barely paid for the English losses in killed and wounded when the little squadron headed northward on the last leg of the Caribbean plunder route and started home. A hurricane caught them just short of the Bahama Strait.

The men around the campfire spoke of the hurricanes as well as the battle, blaming their misfortune on the tremendous force of the wind. It was that which had driven the ships into San Juan de Ulua in practically unnavigable condition. Then the Spaniards in the fort that guarded the harbor trained cannon on them, kept them from leaving.

The place served as anchorage for the immense treasure

fleet which was due to arrive any day from Spain, the English learned. It was near Vera Cruz, where all of the High Mexico wealth and that of the Philippines came on mule-back for shipment every year to the king's treasury at Seville. The English maintained a nervous truce and worked on their damaged vessels until the fleet maneuvered in single file into the roadstead.

There were thirteen Spanish ships, each powerfully armed and well-handled. Even the youngest of the English deck boys making his first voyage began to despair of getting safe out to sea. The English were in a cruel trap, with the fort inland and the huge galleons anchored in close order along the roadstead. Flags of truce were shown and parleys held. Hawkins and Drake were smart enough to keep Spanish officers sent from the fort as hostages.

Peace lasted only until the Spaniards were ready. Don Martin Henriques, the new Viceroy to Mexico, was in the fleet and he gave the fire order. It was a trumpet blast, repeated from ship to ship. The Spanish gunners let go broadsides while the notes still sounded, and English hostages aboard Don Martin's ship were immediately seized and manacled.

Jesus of Lubeck took the worst of the Spanish broadsides. She was pounded so savagely that she lay a hulk, useless. Hawkins managed to abandon her for *Minion*. He was forced to leave some of her people, though; the boat that transferred him was not big enough to take the entire crew.

The memory Job Hortop had of that was very clear. Hawkins had ordered him into the boat. Behind them, men who had been their shipmates for a year pleaded, prayed, cursed, and screamed. One man, a leg gone at the knee, loosened the tourniquet around it, then as the arterial blood gushed, yelled at Hawkins that he would never let the Spaniards take him alive.

Hawkins did not look back. But Hortop recalled the

throb of nerves in the captain's throat and the broken, tortured gasp of his breathing. Nothing was clear after that. It was a confusion of images and actions fused by shock. There was the unremitting crash of cannon, with it the smell of gunpowder, blood, smashed bodies, burning wood, cordage, and canvas.

Hawkins stood on the poop, his knees slightly bent, his hands on his sword belt, and sailed *Minion* through the Spanish fleet and out to sea. He followed his cousin's course in *Judith;* they were a pair of men, Job Hortop thought, whose seamanship could not be matched.

A stiff northerly storm blew outside the roadstead. But *Judith* survived it, clawed offshore, and found running room for herself. *Minion*, battered by the Spaniards, leaking so much that fish were tossed into her hold through the holes in her planking, stayed alive for Hawkins. A night of great misery, Hortop told himself. But one to be proud of, too, and to be remembered.

He grunted at the men who sat beside him in the firelight. They were fools to talk more, he said. They should save their strength for the morning and the march ahead of them. But a couple of the older men, those strong enough to stand up to Hortop, shook their heads and cursed him. The Indians would take care of the party in the morning. The Indians first, and then the Spaniards.

Hortop did not trouble to answer. He lay down in the tangle of grass and shut his eyes, tried to sleep. He succeeded near dawn and awoke to the sun's heat. The other men had gone to the river to drink from the mud-roiled water and wash themselves. Hortop drank with them, his thirst too great for him to hesitate.

They formed an irregular column during the morning and marched inland, keeping near the river. They had no real objective. All they sought, Hortop knew, was capture and an end to their hunger.

The Indians found them as they crossed a savannah. The men in front held out their rolls of trade cloth. They spoke a few words of Spanish, and gestured. But Hortop saw that the Indians carried broad-bladed Spanish knives and wore cheap European britches.

Their manner was instantly surly. They prodded the Englishmen with their bamboo lances, and one of the *Minion* sailors, angry, stepped toward the man who had hurt him. He was shot through the chest with a four-foot, barbed arrow, and died rolling in agony.

The Indians stripped the company bare. They showed no mercy, and still were unbelievably stolid, spoke little, their flat, dark faces expressionless. Their eyes, Hortop thought, seemed to have been made from gun metal, and dully shone.

Hortop was by nature a very patient man. He submitted to the Indians without word or gesture. This, he realized, was just the beginning of many trials. It was going to be a very long passage home.

But the Indians would not let them move without harassment. They struck at some with their spears, and eight were killed, a number more badly wounded. The Englishmen stopped in the narrow trail through the jungle. They turned around toward the Indians, desperate to the point of suicide, determined to fight back empty-handed.

This made no sense, Hortop thought. He strode among the men and restrained them with his huge strength. They had seen him in battle; they could not call him a coward. During the last of the action at San Juan de Ulua, he had fired almost muzzle to muzzle at the Spanish gunners. But here, he warned the men, to fight only made death sure.

He went to the side of the trail, ignoring the Indians

even when they prodded him with spears, and wrenched thick-leaved branches out of the jungle foliage. He gathered ferns that grew shoulder-high and gave them also to his companions. Then he showed the staggering, panting file how to protect their bodies from the sun and the insects. The men covered themselves with the greenery; it helped keep their thought from the Indians.

They followed Hortop on along the trail to the river. Two Spaniards stood on the opposite bank. The Spaniards got into a canoe and crossed and inspected the Englishmen, shouted at the Indians. There was no more molestation, and after the Spaniards returned across the river a force of a hundred cavalrymen appeared. The troops wore steel casques and corselets, and must be stationed, Hortop thought, at a town which could not be far away. The horses had not yet begun to sweat.

Canoes were collected by the Spaniards. The Englishmen were taken over, marched to Panuco under guard of the cavalry. Job Hortop was reluctant to give up the bunch of broad, tall ferns he had used to cover his nakedness. He clung to them in the jail cell after he was given clothing and until he was led away for questioning.

The ferns had taken him far back into memory, restored him to a sense of calm that he would use and cherish for the rest of his life. He was from Bourne, in Lincolnshire, his people among the poorest in the town. A great part of his boyhood was heavily shadowed by hunger. But, when he was five, or six, he had found out on the moors a fen, a wild sort of bog. The sea fowl came there in the spring and fall, and great, fine ferns grew all around it, taller than he was. They were for him a mysterious, delightful forest.

He made a habit of visiting the fen each day of fair weather. He would lie on his back among the ferns, watch the sky, the low-circling birds, the bees, the hornets, and sometimes a wary rabbit. This was his refuge. He retreated to it from the poverty, the hunger, and the meanness of his home.

When he was apprenticed at twelve to Francis Lee, the Queen Majesty's Powdermaker, he took with him in his head the peace of the fen. Lee lived and worked at Redriffe, near London, and often sent his apprentice into the city on errands. Job Hortop learned the powdermaker's trade and a great deal about London, ships, and cannon. Always, though, in the back of his mind was the fen, the birds calling, the sun a shower of light in fragile patterns through the ferns above him, and the wind's gentle music.

The *commandante* at Panuco kept them overnight in the jail, sent them in the morning to Mexico City. That meant a march of more than 300 miles under the blinding, numbing sun. Men died on the road, or fell and could not get up, and were left by the guards. Their companions were given no chance to help; they were driven forward at saber-point by the guards.

So, sagging with weariness, their feet encased within a crust of blood and dust, they came to Mexico City. They were seamen and eternally curious, and they straightened up and stared about them and Hortop remembered for a long time what he saw here. Four hills rose from the wide valley among the sprawl of the canals that held hundreds of canoes carrying fruit, vegetables, flowers, and passengers. Hortop noticed the ruined Indian temples, the new Spanish churches. He saw that there were only two entrances to the city and above them were well-filled watchtowers.

The Englishmen shuffled in through a gate where troops in polished armor stood guard and the officers were mounted. The Englishmen heard themselves called Lutherans, heretical bastards. But they did not give any sign that they understood. They were too weary.

The military authorities interrogated them after their arrival. Then it was the turn of the civilian government, with shrill clerks who asked each man's name several times, and officials who dozed during the sessions. The Englishmen thought that this was comical and made jokes about it at night when they were back in prison. But Job Hortop and some of the other veterans warned them. The interrogations weren't finished; they still had to meet the cunning, sharp-minded priests of the Inquisition.

The priests wanted to know if the Englishmen were good Christians. When they were told, yes, and prayers were recited in Latin, they were satisfied. The group was transferred from prison to a tanner's house, the wounded and the sick sent to various hospitals. The rest regained a lot of their usual, careless gaiety. The dead were gone for good, and there was no more that they could do for the wounded or the sick.

The group was sent to Tescusco, a town about thirty miles from Mexico City. But before they left, Hortop was able to see Robert Barrett, who was the senior English prisoner. Barrett had served as first lieutenant in *Minion,* and gone at Hawkins' request to maintain the truce just before the battle started at San Juan de Ulua. He spoke fluent Spanish, and the Viceroy who knew of his reputation as an officer, kept Barrett a personal prisoner in his palace.

Hortop talked briefly with Barrett. There were sly-eyed servants all around them in the *patio* of the enormous building, and several of them, Hortop was certain, would report to the Viceroy all that was said. Barrett was dressed as a Spanish gentleman, in velvet and lace and fine Cordovan boots. But his face was gaunt with strain, and his dark hair was prematurely gray.

"Tell the lads not to fight," Barrett murmured. "Keep them from it, as you have in the past. 'Tis the only way we shall ever get out alive."

Job Hortop brought his hand to his brow in salute. "Aye, sir," he said. Then he stepped closer and spoke fast. "What chance is there?"

"Some," Barrett said softly. "Some. . . . Be gone now. I can say no more."

Hortop repeated that to the men with whom he went to Tescusco. He told them to keep their tempers, be patient, take any orders which were given them by the Spanish. But that was very difficult, he realized, and gradually accepted the attitude the others held.

Here in the narrow, dirty town with its thick-walled adobe houses built tightly around the central *plaza*, they were treated as slaves, billeted with slaves, and performed slaves' work. Their food was uncooked Indian maize and, at night, a bowl of chick peas with a few peppers. They slept on the stone floor of the shed where all day long they carded wool. Their fellow workers, Indians and Negroes who long since had broken under the Spanish cruelty, started to tremble when the overseer appeared with his steel-tipped lash uncoiled.

Hortop sought refuge in his dream about the fen, but that, he realized, would do him no good now. It was for a time of great crisis, when what the Inquisition priests called his immortal soul was in danger. Other, simpler methods were needed, and the first was outright rebellion against the overseer.

The man was a Spaniard, an illiterate peasant from Galicia. But, like all Spaniards in Mexico, he held himself above any form of manual labor. He was in his own terms a *caballero*, a gentleman, and wore spurs on his round-heeled boots. His assistant wore them, too, although the assistant did not even own a burro. Both men had Indian wives and many children. They talked openly of the day when they would be able to return to Spain and leave all of this behind them.

The Englishmen waited until the overseer's assistant had begun to beat a part-blind Indian. Then they seized him, took away the lash, lowered his britches, and beat him until the blood flowed. He screamed, and the overseer awoke from *siesta* and ran into the carding shed with a pistol lifted.

The Englishmen knocked him down before he could fire it. Job Hortop broke the lock so that it would not operate and tossed it aside. His companions were beating the overseer, taking turns, and only six strokes each. The overseer's mouth was stuffed with raw wool to keep him silent. He was unconscious and so was the assistant when the Englishmen stopped. But it was all they could do to restrain the slaves from killing the pair. The overseer's wife finally came to the door of the shed after dark, looked in and fled and informed the owner of the place.

A great many threats were made. The mayor was called, and the commander of the garrison. But the Englishmen remained firm. They would not work any more, they said, unless they were given better conditions. They refused to be whipped and would not take any further orders from the overseer and his assistant.

The end of it came as Hortop had hoped. The Viceroy was blamed by the people in Tescusco for having sent the heretic dogs here. So he should take them away. The commander of the garrison supplied a messenger who rode to Mexico City with the report of what had happened. When he returned, the Englishmen were told to form a column. Guards surrounded them. They marched back to Mexico City and prison.

Hortop, striding the broad, straight highway, knew that they were extraordinarily lucky. Such luck could not last. They were, all of them, already entered in the records as both pirates and heretics. The Inquisition might at any time turn upon them for much more severe questioning, and afterward there would be torture, possibly the stake.

Job Hortop and some others of the group were kept in Mexico City for two years after that. The rest were taken out of prison, sent down to the coast and to Spain with the *plata* fleet when it made the annual homeward passage. The Inquisition was responsible for the transfer of those men, Job Hortop realized, but whether or not they would be given worse punishment overseas was difficult to guess. Nobody, not even the high-ranking Spanish officers and the heads of the other religious orders could tell what the devious, weird, and terrible minds of the Inquisitors might devise next.

Then all of the Englishmen still in Mexico City, among them Robert Barrett, were sent without warning to the coast. They marched the famous highway down from the high plateau into the steamy *tierra caliente*, passed through Vera Cruz and reached San Juan de Ulua. Chained and fettered, they stood below the fort and gazed across the harbor where they had fought so hard. The memories hurt, and men cursed the Spaniards for breaking the truce.

Robert Barrett told the men to be silent. He said the past was the past, and nothing could be done about it. They should give their thought to getting home.

"When, sir?" one of the *Minion* survivors said.

Barrett said quietly, "I don't know. But Spain is certainly closer than Mexico."

An auxillary vessel attached to the *plata* fleet took them from San Juan de Ulua to Havana. The harbor there was filled with the great, gilded vessels whose long banners and

pennants fluttered close above the water. Staring up, the
Englishmen gauged the waterlines, and Job Hortop realized that the fleet was ready to sail. Then Barrett made a
slight gesture which the gunner understood was meant as
warning.

They were alongside the Admiral-General's vessel, the
flagship. A hard-mouthed Spanish petty officer shouted at
them to get up the ladder and aboard her, fast. Robert Barrett
went first, but he took time as he climbed the ladder to be
very respectful in every way.

Barrett bowed when he reached the main deck. He swept
his plumed hat, given him by the Viceroy, across the sand-
whitened planks, and he answered the officer of the deck in
excellent, easy Spanish. Soldiers who carried half-pikes es-
corted the Englishmen aft and up six flights of ladders and
then in through a doorway that bore above it the coat-of-
arms of imperial Spain.

The Admiral-General was Don Juan de Velasco de
Varre. He sat in a leather chair behind a huge mahogany table
in a cabin where the sunlight from the stern windows pooled
and gleamed. When Robert Barrett bowed, he rose part way
from the chair and inclined his head. He spoke in greeting,
and his glance passed slowly back and forth from Barrett to
the other Englishmen.

Job Hortop watched the Admiral-General in fascination.
This was a man who kept himself aside from many of the
usual hatreds and fixed ideas of war. It showed in the way the
group was greeted and by what he now said. Don Juan asked
them, studying each man's face in turn, would they fight
against their own people if, homeward-bound, the fleet met
English ships at sea.

Barrett answered, and said, "No. But, against the people
of any other nation, we would take your side."

The rest of the group, unhesitating, gave that also as their answer.

Don Juan sat still. Some of his officers, assembled in the fore part of the cabin, stirred nervously, and their sword belts creaked. Then the Admiral-General said that if the Englishmen had answered him in any other way, he would not have believed them. It pleased him to make use of the lot on the passage to Spain. There were never, in any ship of war, he said, enough qualified men.

He called his first lieutenant to stand beside him. Then he told his scribe to read from a document sent by the Viceroy the Englishmen's names and their capacities as seamen. Barrett, a senior officer, was assigned at once to stand watch with the pilot. Job Hortop was assigned to work with the gunners, and William Cawse, an experienced sailor, was to work with the bosun. Another veteran, John Beare, was told to serve as quartermaster. Geoffrey Giles and Edward Rider went with the sailors. Richard, who was down on the list simply as "the master's boy," was put on standby watch with the pilot and Barrett to act as a messenger and to serve them as they saw fit.

The flagship led the fleet out of Havana. The ships were clumsy sailers, slow to answer the helm, and Don Juan put them into single file formation to negotiate the Bahama Strait. They kept under way at night, but in full moonlight, and Job Hortop was down on the foredeck with the watch. Seven decks removed from him, high up on the aftercastle in the almost incredible fashion the Spanish maintained, Robert Barrett paced the quarterdeck with the pilot.

The pilot was the man who was supposed to know these waters, the winds, the currents, the Gulf Stream forces, and the shoals, the many dangers of the mainland shore. Don Juan trusted him completely, put the conduct of the ship in his hands, remained below, and slept. But Job Hortop was uneasy. He remembered the Bahama Strait when the battered little English squadron had tried to sail it before they were beaten back to San Juan de Ulua. He looked out over the leeward bow, to the westward and the mainland. A broad, dark cape named Cañaveral* loomed there.

Hortop knew it. He could place it in his mind. But then he looked down and saw in the breakers close off the bow huge coral heads that would wreck and sink the entire fleet on impact. The Spanish bosun was in charge of the watch on deck. Hortop forgot about him. He was a sailor, too, and he turned, and put his hands to his mouth, and gave a shout with all the power of his lungs behind it.

He told Robert Barrett that this ship and those which followed her were bound for a lee shore, must change course. If they did not come onto the other tack immediately, the fleet was lost.

Barrett took instant action. He did not even consult the pilot. He called his own order to the Spanish bosun. Then, accustomed to taking orders, and very probably having seen the coral heads, the bosun bawled at the watch.

The massive galleon was on the starboard tack, with the wind southeast. Her foresail brace and sheet were slacked, and then her main, and with agonizing slowness for the men who handled her, she came over to the port tack and sheered off from the land. The ships astern steered on the three lanterns on her aftercastle. Those were big enough for a man to crawl inside and contained a dozen tall tapers. But with the night mist on the sea, visibility was poor. There was very little time. The flagship fired a cannon as a signal to the following vessels, warned them to come over at once on the other tack and stand out to sea.

_____
* Now Cape Kennedy.

Don Juan climbed the ladders from his cabin on the run. The sudden change of course and the lurching of the ship told him of the danger. When he had listened to the leadsmen who sounded the water from the bow chains, and to the look-outs in the mast tops, then looked overside at the white crest of breakers along the coral and the loom of the cape, his anger burst. He asked some very pointed questions of the pilot, and got vague, halting answers. So he talked with the quartermaster at the helm, summoned the bosun from the foredeck.

He listened to them carefully, and thanked them. Then he crossed the deck and stood beside Robert Barrett. He thanked Barrett for what he had done, told the man that his prompt action and Job Hortop's had saved the entire fleet. And as for the pilot, he was going to be hanged in the morning. Twice before, by his faulty navigation, the pilot had almost wrecked the fleet.

Barrett thanked Don Juan, and at the end of the watch took care to seek out Job Hortop in the crew's quarters. The Spanish sailors had heard of what had happened. A wineskin was produced by the bosun, and all hands had a drink, and the pilot was vigorously described. Then, with dawn, a signal cannon was fired, and the other admiral in the fleet came alongside the flagship in his vessel.

He was Don Diego Flores de Valdes, and Don Juan wanted him to witness the hanging of the pilot. But Don Diego did not agree with Don Juan. He told the Admiral-General that he did not think the pilot should be hanged. Let the man have another chance, Don Diego said. This was a difficult passage for any navigator.

Job Hortop stood in the waist of the flagship and listened with great surprise. These were very high-ranking Spaniards who argued, and both believed in mercy, because

at last Don Juan agreed. He would give the pilot another
chance, and keep the man at his job.

The fleet took its regular formation and shaped a north-
easterly course for a landfall on the Azores. The pilot's work
was better; the island of Fayal was picked up at his estimated
time of arrival. Then, heading eastward, on the last leg of the
voyage, with Seville only a couple of weeks away, the Spaniards celebrated.

It was the feast day of St. James, the most popular on
the Spanish religious calendar. The trumpeters sounded, and
the ship's musicians played. Special food and wine rations
were ordered. Fireworks were lit at dusk. The crew danced
the decks with rachets in their hands, and brandishing pin-
wheels. They accepted the Englishmen fully as their shipmates and made them join in the fun.

Robert Barrett stayed away from most of the celebration,
though. He was aware that for him and his companions only
a very small amount of time remained. They were certain
to be subjected to rigorous, lengthy examination by the Inquisition when the fleet reached Spain. Leniency had been
shown in Mexico and aboard ship. That would not continue
in Spain. Their luck would run out when they were brought
before the chief Inquisitors in Seville.

Job Hortop was the man Barrett talked with first. He
waited until a rain squall had sent the celebrants below and
he could meet Hortop in a dark corner of the foredeck. Then
he spoke rapidly, trusting Hortop to understand each word.
Hortop nodded in agreement. It must be tried, he said. There
would be little chance for any of them in Spain.

Hortop explained the plan to John Beare. The quartermaster passed it on until, singly, the six men and the boy,
Richard, were informed. They promised to be ready to take
part in the attempt to escape.

The fleet was still abreast of the Azores, held a course near the island of Terceira. This ship was the only one to tow a pinnace astern. They could slip down the towline in the darkness with a jug of water and a sack of bread. Then they would sail for Terceira and hide themselves in a cove. There should be a fair chance after that of a passage home to England.

Hortop stole a sack from the bosun's locker. The group gave him their bread crusts and he put those in it, hid the sack again in the locker. Then Richard managed to steal and fill a large water jug. Hortop reported to Barrett in a quick meeting on a ladder. The next night at midnight, Barrett said. He had a small hand compass, borrowed from the master gunner. They were ready to leave.

But the master gunner, while he had given Barrett the compass, suspected him. He went to the Admiral-General and told him of the loan. Don Juan put Barrett under arrest at once, confined him in stocks with heavy iron ballast bars set across his legs. Hortop and the others were seized in their quarters or on watch and confined in the same way as Barrett.

Don Juan ordered the ship's mainsail set aback. She was stopped in the water and a signal cannon was fired. Then the pinnace went around the fleet and collected Don Diego Flores de Valdes and all of the senior officers. They boarded Don Juan's ship for a council just as the main yard was lowered to deck, and special blocks rigged from it. Don Juan proposed to hang the English prisoners.

He told the assembled officers that the Englishmen had fomented a plot. Powder trains were to be laid to the magazine and then fired at the very last minute before the plotters shoved off in the pinnace. He asked the council to agree to the death sentence as the penalty.

Don Diego objected. He held practically equal rank with Don Juan, had been in command of that part of the *plata* fleet which had gone to Porto Bello on the Panamanian isthmus to pick up treasure. His argument against the death sentence was rather subtle, and the Englishmen heard about it later from Spanish petty officers who were their friends and served as orderlies at the council.

Don Diego said it would look quite strange when the fleet reached Spain for a report to be made which told of a plot by six men and a boy to steal this ship's pinnace and get away in her. He would have plotted in the same way if he were among the English, and their attempt was only logical. So he would not vote for the death sentence, nor, he was certain, would any of the captains, mates, and pilots gathered here. Let the Englishmen live. They should stay in irons until they could be turned over to the civil authorities and tried by a tribunal at the *Casa de Contratacion* at Seville.

Don Diego stood up then and bowed to Don Juan and wished him good sailing for the rest of the voyage. He motioned slightly to the other officers. They rose, bowing and murmuring politely, followed Don Diego down the ladders to the main deck and the boat ladder. Don Juan sat silent for a while, afterward gave an order for the main yard to be hoisted and sail set, and for the prisoners to be kept secure on the same rations of bread and water.

Their good fortune at sea sustained the English group for the next year. They passed it in the wet-walled and almost lightless dungeons of the *Casa de Contratacion*, the immense structure in Seville which acted as a headquarters for colonial affairs and as a prison. Some of them abandoned hope toward the end of that time, but not Hortop, and not Barrett.

The gunner kept his courage while rats sidled close to him in the cell where he lay fettered. Men driven mad by the agony of the Inquisition racks screamed, and against the subterranean wall of the prison, the tide surge of the Guadalquivir River swept in flow and ebb.

Barrett received word from outside. He passed it to the others through a turnkey who had been bribed. Hawkins and Drake were back in England with what was left of their crews after the bitterly cruel homeward passage. Queen Elizabeth had made Hawkins an admiral, and he was busy keeping his word to the castaways. There was an escape plan for them here that was almost ready.

Hortop knew that there were Englishmen here in Seville who held power at court. They were from Catholic merchant families who had lived in Spain for generations, and through them Hawkins might arrange many things. But the Inquisition's spies were everywhere, and the Inquisition ran the country, not the king.

Then, in darkness, without word, the turnkey came to Hortop in his cell and released him from his fetters. Hortop rose, suddenly eager, trembling, panting, thinking of sunlight, and all that freedom meant. He met the others in the passage outside the cell. Barrett led them. Barrett seemed to be supremely confident.

But in a side street past the *Casa de Contratacion* a patrol met them. They fought hard against the halbardiers. Hortop stood with Barrett and gave time to their companions. They were weak from the prison months, though, and Hortop and Barrett and men named John Gilbert and Humphrey Roberts and John Emery were caught.

They went back to their same cells in the *Casa de Contratacion*. Twelve tides passed; Hortop counted them, unable to summon the dream of the fen, oppressed by an overpowering sense of dread. The Englishmen were transferred to the main city prison and from that to the dungeons at Triana which were used solely for confinement of prisoners held by the Inquisition.

The incarceration there lasted a year. They were interrogated, tortured, allowed to recoup from festering wounds in their cells, interrogated and questioned further, flung back into the cells. Strength persisted for them, though, and a degree of hope. They could stand upright when they were taken out from the dungeons to a courtyard and given the sanbenito to wear.

They knew the meaning of the coarse brown garment with the yellow St. Andrew's cross upon it. This was the beginning of an Inquisition procession which would bring them to the scaffold, the stake. Candles were put in their hands, and they marched forth in the sunlight with the pigeons swooping and came to the great main *plaza* of St. Francis where the crowd had already formed.

The guards pushed them up onto the high scaffold in the center. They were told to sit on benches, each in his allotted place. Another scaffold was opposite them. The men who sat there were judges and priests and the principal officers of the Inquisition.

Job Hortop turned his head and looked at the stakes. They were of green wood, thick, tall; faggots had been piled around them, and the body chains hung ready. Here it was, he thought. Aye, at last. And of them, which would go to the burning?

He gazed at Robert Barrett and saw death in Barrett's face, but with it a calmness. He remembered that years ago in Mexico, because of his knowledge of Spanish, Barrett had acted as interpreter for some of the Englishmen. He had parried the Inquisitors' questions, and twisted the meanings, made jokes that caused his companions to laugh. But some of the Inquisitors understood English; it had been marked against

Barrett's record—while the saving of the treasure fleet had been forgotten.

A pale and smooth-faced priest was in the pulpit on the other scaffold. He preached for two hours while in the crowd fruit and meat and wine were sold. People shouted at the prisoners. Some said they should go free. Others wanted to burn the heretics right away.

Bresinia, the Secretary of the Inquisition, took the priest's place and the crowd was silent. He held a long document in his hands and Hortop knew that it was the process, contained the sentences for those who had been found guilty. Hortop locked his teeth. He asked himself if he was ready to die among the flames.

But men who took orders from Bresinia, familiars of the Inquisition, moved along the row of benches to Robert Barrett and John Gilbert. They marched them to the other scaffold to stand in front of Bresinia. Those two would burn, Hortop realized, and felt a sweat of horror down his throat and chest.

Bresinia read the sentence while the familiars stood close beside Barrett and Gilbert. There was no more now except the actual agony. The prisoners were taken to the stakes and chained. The flames began to rise.

Gilbert screamed once or twice. It was Hortop's belief that Barrett kept silent. But he was not certain. Hortop had tried once more to hide within his dream of the fen. The dream, too, became fiery, birds fell from overhead and were consumed; flame wrapped him, and he died the same death as his shipmate, Robert Barrett.

It was only when a familiar jerked him upright by his fetter chain from the bench that he realized he was still alive. He looked blankly at the familiar and obeyed the man, stumbled from the scaffold. John Bone was beside him, and they were being pushed toward the other scaffold. A sweat of fear was on Bone's face, but he swabbed it off with the sleeve of his sanbenito. Hortop admired him for that. He stood straight, too, when they halted before Bresinia to hear their sentence read.

They were sentenced to the galleys, would serve as oarsmen for ten years apiece. Then they would be returned to Seville, wear the sanbenito, and spend the rest of their lives in prison. Another pair of Englishmen, Thomas Ellis and John Marks, received a sentence of eight years in the galleys. Humphrey Roberts and John Emery, called in their turn, were given five years apiece.

Hortop had been returned by the familiars to his place on the bench on the other scaffold. He glanced around, silently saying the words of farewell to Barrett. But the fires were out; the chains hung empty. A pigeon came to rest on the charred stake. Hortop shut his eyes. This did no good. He started to think about the galleys, and how he would survive them, finally get free, and go home to England.

He served twelve years at the galley sweeps, two more than his sentence, and those for what an overseer considered mutinous action. He and the other oarsmen were chained in groups of four to a sweep. They lived on an unchanging ration of biscuit and water. They were issued each year two shirts and two pairs of trousers made from sail canvas, and a loose red surcoat and a cape of rough wool with a hood. Their heads and beards were shaved once a month. They slept on the thwarts where they rowed, and the floorboards were their toilets. The officers in command of the galleys carried canes with perfume sacks in the hollow ends. The overseers, graduates of the rowing thwarts, used the lash with intense satisfaction.

Hortop finished his service and went back to Seville, the

sanbenito, and prison. But John Hawkins still remembered him. Money was paid to various people—just how Hortop did not know. He only wore the sanbenito for four years, though, and then he went to work for Hernando de Soria, the treasurer of the royal mint. When he had worked for de Soria for seven years as a servant, his employer lent him fifty ducats and arranged a court hearing. Hortop paid the exact sum and was allowed to take off the sanbenito.

Hope came back to him despite all that had happened. He realized that a man as powerful as de Soria would not help him and lend him money without very good reason. Hortop wore the simple clothing of a Spanish servant, and spoke the language without accent. He left Seville in October, 1590, was not stopped on his way to the coast.

There were Flemish seamen who made their homes in the port of San Lucar. They were married to Spanish women and sailed regularly offshore in a coaster they owned. Hortop reached them. An agreement was made. They were taking to sea a contraband cargo of salt and wine. Hortop went with them in their vessel.

A sea rendezvous was kept with an English galleon named *Dudley*. She took aboard the cargo and the captain accommodated Hortop. He landed at Portsmouth on December 2, 1590, asked his way to the quarters of the King's Lieutenant.

He was received, greeted, and questioned. The King's Lieutenant then sent him on to London and the Earl of Sussex. The questioning was repeated, but with much more detail. It was Christmas Eve when Hortop finished his report.

He started for Redriffe, and was not sure of his welcome. It was twenty-three years since he had been in England.

"The night came on, dreadful beyond description, in which, attempting to throw out our topsails to claw off the shore, they were immediately blown from the yards."

This was written years after shipwreck and terrible loss of life at the end of a Cape Horn passage in 1741 by HMS Wager. *It was part of the "Narrative" of Vice Admiral John Byron, known throughout the Royal Navy for his vicissitudes at sea as "Foul Weather Jack."*

His grandson, Lord George Gordon Byron, took from it the shipwreck scenes for the epic poem, "Don Juan." He referred to the Admiral's account as "My Grand-Dad's Narrative."

JOHN BYRON

*T*HE WIND, suddenly veering, came out of the southward. That was the direction of Antarctica and the South Pole, and there was enormous force in the gusts. *Wager* trembled under them, refused her helm, and fell off course with the wind. Then the tide caught her and she started to bear down upon the jagged rocks of the shore.

John Byron as midshipman of the watch stood in the leeward mizzen rigging and checked the distance through a long glass. Right beyond, no more than a mile away, was Staten Land. The ship would pile up there unless she could claw off and regain her course. But *Wager* was old, slow, and very heavily laden. Byron was still in his teens and had been going to sea for only a short time; he was tempted to pray.

Captain Cheap was on the quarterdeck, though, and called a series of sharp orders through the wind screech. *Wager* was put on the other tack. She answered gradually, swung offshore, was once more safely headed toward the Pacific through the windings of Le Maire Strait.

Byron felt proud of her. She was the oldest ship in the squadron of seven that had started out from England in the early spring of 1740 to sail around the world and seize Spanish treasure anywhere along the way. Captain George Anson, who commanded the squadron, had designated her as the stores ship. She was a former East Indiaman, built for cargo-carrying, and the people at the Portsmouth Navy Yard had stowed her with all that she could take. She carried various kinds of careening gear for the squadron's use, and supplies of powder and shot, provisions, bales of merchandise for trade in the Pacific islands, paint, tar, hawsers, cables, and her own full equipment, including some very bulky cannon.

Byron did not think much of her ability to use the cannon. She was too deep in the water for the main, broadside batteries to be brought to bear with real efficiency. And most of the gunners and the rest of the crew were sick or decrepit. They had been discharged as invalids from Chelsea Hospital only to be sent aboard here.

Byron got down out of the rigging and crossed the deck to Captain Cheap. The captain was unwell, had been suffering with fever ever since the squadron had left the Brazilian coast and headed for Cape Horn. He leaned yellow-faced against the quarterrail, his hands gripping the mahogany, his eyes in strained contemplation of the sea. Byron started to speak and offer the captain his arm. Then he, too, saw in the flurries of spindrift from off the wave crests the vast, hollowly curving wave that toppled black and mountainous high above all the rest.

Captain Cheap released his grip on the rail. He took his speaking trumpet from under his arm and shouted at the watch down in the waist of the ship. It was a warning; he told the men to run for their lives.

The wave boarded *Wager* just below the crosstrees. John Byron was flung backward, battered, choked, and nearly drowned. He fetched up in the lee scuppers beside Captain Cheap. The captain had lost the speaking trumpet, his hat, wig, and sword. He cursed with some of the most obscene phrases that Byron had ever heard.

Byron helped the captain to his feet. He pretended not to notice that Captain Cheap was completely bald. But then he was very busy carrying out the captain's orders. The entire mizzenmast, shrouds, running rigging, sails and all, had been carried away out of the ship. The windward-side chain plates, made of stout iron straps, were snapped off short. The steersman stood swaying at the tiller, shocked past intelligence.

Byron took the helm from him as the first of the captain's orders, fought the ship back onto her course. He looked forward and saw that Mr. Jones, the mate, had sent the watch to the pumps to clear the water from her. Captain Cheap was staring at the other ships, dimly visible in column formation off the bow. He told Byron to keep in line with them, follow them through the strait. Then he disappeared below.

It was too cold here on deck for a baldheaded man, Byron thought. The captain needed either another wig or a hat. It was soon going to be too cold also for a soaking-wet midshipman. He pounded his hands on the tiller haft for warmth, and abruptly, up through the rudder stock, felt the vibration as the wind shifted and increased.

This might be the first of a series of the dreaded westerly gales, Byron thought. He steadied the helm and kept the ship from yawing as Mr. Jones sent the watch to trim sail. Captain

Cheap emerged from the companionway with a tricorne hat pushed down against his ears. Forward, on the somber horizon where the rest of the squadron labored, Byron noticed that the ships had taken in their topsails. So it was gale all right, and might last for days.

He was relieved at the tiller by a new steersman soon after darkness. He changed into dry clothing and convinced the surgeon that he deserved a drink of rum for medicinal purposes. The surgeon was generous, and Byron felt both sleepy and lazy. He greatly regretted his name being shouted by a messenger.

The captain wanted him on deck, the messenger said. This was a call for all hands. Gale was making up and the ship was about to go under bare poles. Byron finished the rum, thanked the surgeon, and went on deck.

The gales blew steadily for a week. *Wager* suffered more damage, partly unmanageable with her mizzen gone. Her carpenter was over aboard *Gloucester*, one of the other ships in the squadron, and for some days the severity of the weather would not let him return. Waves swept *Wager* fore and aft. She lost several of her boats; they were smashed in their lashings by swift-reaching seas, the fragments tossed overboard in the recoil.

Captain Cheap ordered a jury mizzenmast rigged so that the ship could be headed closer to the wind and eased. Byron worked with the bosun's gang while a lower studdingsail boom was set up as a mast, and temporary shrouds rigged to support it. But *Wager* still rode very hard in the storm welter. They were forced to jettison a bower anchor to ease the foremast. The foremast shrouds were torn away, and the fore chain plates broken. Byron, writing years later about that, reported in his "Narrative" the ship was "in all parts in a most crazy condition."

Still, Captain Cheap tried to make good the course that had been ordered for all of the ships in the squadron. It had been decided weeks ago that they should keep a rendezvous at Socoro Island, then proceed up the west coast of South America for an attack upon the port of Baldivia. Necessary stores for the attack were aboard *Wager*, and Captain Cheap drove her hard toward the rendezvous.

His officers pointed out the danger of the course he held and were reminded that they were his subordinates and this was the Royal Navy. He was in command; they were to obey him or be considered mutinous. John Byron listened in respectful silence, glad that he was only a midshipman and was not forced to make his belief known to the captain.

Byron swarmed up into the mizzen rigging and used his shirt tail to clean the salt rime from the long glass lens. Then he saw off the bow land birds that swooped over the wave crests, and yellow patches of seaweed, and a tall, dark headland. He hailed the deck and reported land close on the larboard bow.

Captain Cheap came into the rigging and took the long glass from him. He treated Byron to a few of his more vehement curses. *Wager*, he said, was bound straight for a lee shore. Byron agreed to that; he could see the white, ominous toss of breakers along the headland. Then Captain Cheap sent him to the foredeck to give a hand with the watch.

The iron straps that supported some of the blocks aloft broke without warning and let the yard crash thumping down from the mast. The watch ran for safety, their hands over their heads, and John Byron dived for a bulwark, crouched beneath it. The men were very tired, some of them weakened by scurvy, and others too frightened to work aloft. It was some time before the yard was rigged again and hauled aloft, then the foresail set.

Wager wore around, her head to the southward, and the men of the watch clapped each other on the back, and on the quarterdeck Captain Cheap no longer stood rigid with tension. But the wind velocity was increasing. The old ship labored, rolled, took vast quantities of water aboard. John Byron hunched in the lee of the foredeck. Water was knee-deep in his seaboots; he was miserable, chilled numb, and profoundly frightened.

This was the worst storm yet, he knew. It was gathering intensity with darkness, and here on deck were only twelve men who were fit to work the ship. The bosun had tucked the end of his beard inside his sailcloth jacket to keep it out of his way. He moved from man to man and repeated the order until all of them understood. They were to bend on the topsails, and if they failed, the ship would certainly be driven ashore.

The coarse hemp topsails were set, and trimmed carefully to the wind. The wind struck them in single, final blows and they were gone, small tatters flapping momentarily from the bolt ropes. There was nothing more to be done. The bosun told the men to get aft, and they climbed up the ladder to the quarterdeck.

Captain Cheap rested head down beside the leeward rail. He had hurt himself while helping with the foreyard repair work, and was in considerable pain. John Byron moved close to him. He hoped to hear the captain give an order that would save the ship.

The hour glass had just been turned. It was four o'clock, near dawn. Another hour now, and there would be enough light to maneuver. Captain Cheap was a very skillful navigator. He could find a way to take *Wager* offshore.

But then the ship went aground. She shivered in her length, her beams ends lurching rapidly over into the leap of the breakers. There were men below who were confined to their bunks by scurvy. When the ship righted partly, Byron was given a lanthorn by Mr. Jones, the mate, and sent to look for them. He found the bodies face down, arms outstretched, bumping from bulkhead to bulkhead with the motion of the ship.

He returned to deck as fast as he could climb. Men who had protested for more than two months that they were unfit for duty jostled him. They had abruptly found their strength and wanted him to tell them what the captain had done to the ship. Byron remembered some of the captain's epithets. He expressed himself to the recently sick, then sprinted across the quarterdeck.

Mr. Jones had taken over command of the ship. She had sheered off the rocks after the initial impact, lay clear, all headway gone from her. Now she struck, hurled by the wind, and with immense force. John Byron heard the rudder crack and smash, saw in the dim predawn light the steersman fall headlong on deck as the tiller pitched him.

Mr. Jones mustered all hands on the quarterdeck. The steersman got to his feet and grasped the tiller, although it gave almost no control. Mr. Jones was shouting to the men in a voice stronger than the storm sounds. He told them how to handle the braces and the sheets so that those steered the ship and brought her in past the first line of breakers.

Some of the men began to cheer, and then the ship hit once more, heavily, her bottom planking smashed, her masts bucking in wild spirals against the shrouds, blocks torn away aloft, yards, sheets, braces, halyards inextricably fouled. This was the last time, John Byron realized. *Wager* could take no more. Captain Cheap and Mr. Jones had done their best.

The mate was stubborn, though, and went down into the waist of the ship with the carpenter. They took axes and chopped away the foremast, let it lop overboard to ease the ship. Then they cut the mainmast out of her. But the effect was not much, Byron saw. He blinked his wind-burned eyes and stared at the shore. It was close. *Wager* was well inside the barrier reef.

The men of the crew were openly frightened as they looked at the ship in the dawn light, then at the shore. Several of them said harshly that the ship was finished. They would never live to get ashore. Waves still beat over the vessel, combed across her waist, slammed upon the hatches and flung in swift, vicious rushes along the quarterdeck.

Men who suffered from scurvy sat slack, their strength gone, and were caught by the sea and drowned. The religious knelt and prayed, but did not keep their handholds. They were swept away, helpless, mouths open in surprise. Horror was too much for some of the rest; they went insane. One sailor shouted into the wind that he was "king of the country." He held a cutlass and he walked the quarterdeck swinging and jabbing with the blade.

John Byron watched Mr. Jones. The mate crouched down when a wave retreated from the deck, then tackled the man who waved the cutlass. Mr. Jones sent him prone, and Byron stamped on the blade with his seaboot heel, then tossed the broken weapon over the side. The man lay unconscious, but Byron did not have enough time to secure him with a rope end before the next wave came aboard.

Mr. Jones was shouting from the forward side of the deck. He told Byron to join him and Lieutenant Hamilton. The young Royal Marine officer had a pistol in each hand. He gave one to Byron and indicated the main deck.

The bosun and some of the sailors had ventured there. They drew out the battens, lifted the tarpaulins. Then they opened the hatch and reached down right after the onrush of a wave. Brandy casks had been pressed upward by the water that entered the hold through the smashed hull planks. The bosun wanted brandy and knew how to get it. He laughed and made mocking gestures at the officers as he filled a pannikin.

John Byron was very conscious of the fact that he belonged among the officer group. These men down on the main deck were mutineers, carried a deep hatred for him and his kind. There was reason for their hatred, too, and he understood it. They were rarely paid, poorly fed, subjected to the lash and many forms of savage discipline, kept in the navy ships for years without shore leave.

Now this lot, gulping brandy by the pannikin, was drunk. They entered the quarters below and broke into sea-chests and lockers, looted, argued, and fought with each other, stumbled back on deck to pour another pannikin. When they slipped and fell, many of them drowned there beside the hatch, ignored by men who could still duck the waves.

Mr. Jones said that it was time to leave the ship. He gave Byron permission to go to the wardroom. There were "some little matters," Byron said, that he would like to take from his sea-chest. But the wardroom was partly awash, and the ship was in such agony that he came back topside empty-handed.

The mate nodded at him in understanding and said to get the boat ready for shore. Captain Cheap, his dislocated shoulder tightly bound, was in his bunk. He was carried wrapped in blankets to the boat and the boat lowered away with a large group aboard. Byron made the first run to the beach, took command of the craft after the people landed from her, went to the ship for another load.

He kept a count of those he ferried ashore, and it was

145 men. The rest, the mutineers, who were about ten men and were led by the bosun, jeered and yelled and waved weapons. But they did nothing to harm Byron, and on his last trip, when he asked them if they wanted to go ashore, they only laughed and patted the brandy cask.

Byron regretted that he had not taken a drink with them. The shore was bleak, and there was no food, no heat. Lieutenant Hamilton had found a deserted Indian hut in the woods beyond the beach. But it was too small to accommodate more than a few of the party. The storm still blew with fierce velocity; fire was impossible in the rain. The men huddled together, and during that night three of them, one a lieutenant, died of exposure.

Byron sat sleepless. He thought of London and home and a brightly glowing fire in the drawing-room grate. A footman brought another bucketful of coal and carefully spilled some on while his mother continued her crochet and his father never looked up from his newspaper. Smells of cooking rose from the kitchen in the basement. Leg of lamb. And plum pudding. Cook had started the pudding early in the afternoon and given him a sample.

Byron drove the dream from his mind. Stuff such as that was a waste of time, he told himself. It only stole from a man's energy, and undermined his courage. Byron lifted his head to the wind and the rain and laughed. He had just put himself among the grown men. There was no excess pride in that, though. He had proven his right to it out to sea, when the jury mizzenmast had been rigged, and in the way he handled the boat between the ship and the beach. He was just barely in the officer class, the lowest-ranking of the lot. Nobody could deny, though, that he was a real sailor, and was qualified to take responsibility.

The day when it broke was worse than the night.

Hunger increased, and while the rain stopped and fire was made, there was no food. Men walked the rocky beach, looking for crayfish, limpets, bird eggs, anything that might be edible. Captain Cheap lay in his sodden blankets in the little hut and told John Byron to start a record of what happened here.

The shipwreck had been on May 14, at approximately five o'clock in the morning. This was Socoro Island, and as well as he could remember the chart, Captain Cheap said, it was 90 leagues North of the westerly entrance of the Straits of Magellan. The latitude was between forty-seven and forty-eight degrees South.

Captain Cheap asked what it looked like outside. Byron explained that they were camped at the foot of a bay formed by steep promontories. The one directly to the northward rose high from the sea, and he was tempted to call that Mount Misery. There was a pair of big lagoons in sight to the northward, too, and beyond them a huge range of mountains.

Captain Cheap told him that without doubt the mountains were part of the main cordillera that ran the length of the South American continent. *Wager* had almost completed her westing into the Pacific when the storm put her ashore. Captain Cheap grimaced with hunger as he spoke. Nobody had eaten solid food for days. Storm conditions had stopped all cooking efforts. He asked Byron now if the men who walked the beach succeeded in finding food.

Byron's own hunger pangs made him stoop when he left the hut. The men had found nothing except a coarse kind of weed that one of them said could be eaten if boiled. The fire on the beach was fanned, and rain water heated in a pannikin. Handfuls of the weed were tossed in along with bits of tallow from candles.

Captain Cheap got up while the stuff was cooked. He left

the hut and stood beside the fire. The first soup taken from the fire was offered to him. He drank it and almost immediately vomited. But the hunger of the others was too great. They all drank, and all were violently sick.

While they crouched twitching with pain the mutineer group came ashore from the ship. The bosun led it, extremely drunk, yet able to steer the boat and keep erect on the beach. He and the other mutineers wore gold-laced officers' coats over their dirty, checked cotton shirts and tar-splotched trousers. They were armed with cutlasses, pistols, and a couple of muskets.

John Byron forgot his stomach trouble. He moved gradually back from the fire until he stood with Captain Cheap and Lieutenant Hamilton. The Royal Marine officer had brought the captain's cane from the hut. He held a brace of pistols, but beneath his coattails, out of sight of the bosun and the bosun's companions.

The bosun staggered, yelling at the captain. He said that he was going to cut Captain Cheap's head off, and about time, too. Captain Cheap told the bosun to come closer and go right on with the head-cutting. Lieutenant Hamilton muttered to John Byron to draw his dirk and use it when and if necessary.

The bosun had approached too close to Captain Cheap. The captain delivered a blow of the cane that was so fast Byron hardly saw it. A low cry of surprise came from the bosun. He reeled, and his beard bobbed high as his head jerked with the blow, and then he lay unconscious.

Lieutenant Hamilton showed the brace of pistols. He spoke quietly to the other mutineers. It was not his practice, he said, to shoot former shipmates. But this lot should get back aboard the wreck before they made him enforce simple caution. The men cursed him. Several started forward with their cutlasses poised. Then they halted; their anger ebbed and became noisy protest. They dragged the bosun away, went to their boat, back to the wreck.

His dirk still in his hand, John Byron felt tremendous relief. He had worked on deck in the storm with most of those men. The bosun had months ago shown him how to make a long splice, and to sew canvas, find his way around aloft. Hamilton's caution was all very well, but shipmates counted, too.

Then Captain Cheap spoke to him. The party was in possession of both the ship's cutter and her yawl. The yawl, cast loose from the ship, had floated ashore and was still in good shape. It was time the party here armed themselves. The Indians who had built this hut might return, and they were known to be unfriendly.

John Byron got the impression that the captain wished him to volunteer to take the yawl out to the wreck and bring back a supply of arms and ammunition. He drew himself up as straight as his stomach condition would permit and proposed that he take command of the yawl for the purpose Captain Cheap indicated.

It was grisly work with the yawl. Sea-torn bodies were floating in the shallows where she was anchored. When he had recruited a couple of sailors and put the yawl under way toward the wreck, more bodies were encountered. Birds rode some of those, and pecked at the eyes, the mouths, the distended bellies. Out at the wreck, the mutineers mumbled, stupid with rum, and across the main deck, body shoved body in the backwash of the subsiding storm.

Byron refused to board the wreck, or let the men with him board her. His caution came from the fact that only her forecastle and her quarterdeck were free from the sea. He told the yawl crew to use long grapnel hooks and haul from the decks and cabins and storerooms whatever could be reached. They returned several times to the wreck, and the mutineers offered them no resistance.

When darkness came, Byron secured the yawl off the beach. He took the sails ashore. All of the untrustworthy men, he told himself, weren't aboard the wreck. The cutter had been hauled up past high tide mark by a group the carpenter and the chief gunner led. Props were chopped from tree limbs to support her on her side, and a canvas shelter made that reached to the ground. The stores and various articles that Byron's crew had brought ashore in the yawl were neatly stowed there. But pilfering started right away; holes were cut in the canvas, or a corner was plucked loose from the stones that held it in place.

Lieutenant Hamilton stopped that. He used the flat of his sword and a pistol butt. Then he posted a guard at the stores shed and put Byron in command of it. Byron borrowed a pistol from him and thrust the barrel through his belt. He had felt a sense of sympathy for the men aboard the wreck when he had been there during the day. They were marked for death, he realized. When the brandy was gone, life would soon end for them through some careless or wanton act. And it might be that they held hidden in their thought the wish to die, to get away from this desolate and terrible place.

Men were blundering along the beach in the darkness. They said they looked for fish, for mussels and sea birds. Some of those had been found there during the day, but not enough to feed the full complement. Now the search was for the buzzards that sat on the corpses left stranded by the tide. Violent fights began. They were too violent, Byron thought, for the possession of a skinny, brine-soaked buzzard. Then he heard the shouts called back and forth, and realized that the men were accusing each other of cannibalism. Mention was made of arms and legs that were gone from corpses.

Byron felt nausea. He stood shuddering. Sweat broke out on his brow. But then the nausea changed to rage.

There had been a swift red gash of crimson from the dim loom of the wreck. He ducked instinctively and went almost prone. That was a quarterdeck cannon which had been fired, he knew. The mutineers, drunk as they might be, could still handle a piece. With a screech that told him it was very close, the eighteen-pound ball passed overhead, cleared the top of the stores shed, and went caroming among the trees beyond the beach.

Byron cursed the mutineers. It did not matter, he thought, whether or not he was an officer. First, last, he wanted to get out of here alive. And with a bit of honor left. Yes, honor. A man who ate his shipmates' flesh could not be called honorable.

But Byron laughed. He was using words he had heard at home in London. They belonged to the upper class, to the people who had the money to buy the commissions for their sons, send them out well-placed into the navy, the army, the marines. He had never felt acute hunger until after *Wager* piled ashore here; he had never stood beneath the lash the bosun's mate dealt with great, brute pleasure. John Byron was a very lucky fellow, very lucky indeed.

The man who had just begun to cut the canvas of the stores shed with a bayonet point was clumsy in his haste. Byron heard him and saw him. He lifted Lieutenant Hamilton's pistol and cocked it, took aim. He told the pilferer to drop the bayonet and then stand still or he would shoot him dead.

The man rested motionless after he dropped the bayonet. He wept, and told Byron that he was hungry. But Byron remembered the shouts on the beach, and the cannon shot delivered from the wreck. He found a piece of rope and lashed the man tightly to a pole, went to get Lieutenant Hamilton and make sure that punishment was given for this crime.

The Indians arrived the next day, entering through the reef in three canoes. They were small and very swarthy. Their lank, black hair hung low across their flat-featured faces. Shawls made of bird feathers were around their shoulders; the men wore leather breechclouts cut from sheep-skin. The Englishmen vigorously used sign language and tried to describe sheep, even uttered baaing noises.

The Indians seemed to fail to understand. They said nothing and got back in their canoes and went away to the eastward. The people on the beach were given to almost total despair, and were so weak that it was difficult for them to move.

Men began to die every day. The bodies were taken away at last by the tide.

John Byron kept himself occupied by trips out to the wreck. He often sailed the yawl single-handed, led the jib and mizzen sheets into the cockpit where he could handle them with the main sheet. The bosun blinked at him vacant-eyed from the quarterdeck of *Wager*. He held no animosity for Byron, and pitched down into the yawl a small fowling piece and a bag of powder and shot for it.

His lot were going away soon, the bosun said, mumbling the words. They were about to finish a canoe, hollowed out of the mainmast timber. Very good craft. Take them where they wanted to go.

Byron remembered when this bloated, shaky-handed man was a superb sailor, and that was no more than three weeks ago. He had been very proud then to get the bosun's praise for the work he did on deck. Now he felt only pity. He asked the bosun, where would they go in the canoe?

The bosun indicated the rock-shouldered headlands to the eastward. That way. After the Indians. It would do no good to try to buck the prevailing westerlies.

Byron kept silent. He could not hold the bosun back from death, he knew. He pushed the yawl's bow clear from the wreck, trimmed sail, came about, and ran the boat for the beach.

Men there had been watching him while he talked with the bosun. They wanted to look at the fowling piece and borrow it. He pushed past them, ready to fight, and went off into the woods behind the hut that Captain Cheap and some of the other senior officers occupied.

Byron had started building some weeks ago a small lean-to for his own use deep in the woods. He had worked on it when free from his boat-handling. It offered him a haven where he could be alone, get away from the tragedy, the misery, the constant sight of death. The original count had been 145 men taken from the wreck. It was now an even hundred, and by dawn it would be less.

He looked around him to see that he was not followed, then entered the lean-to. He put down the fowling piece and clapped his hands and whistled. The dog was still shy, but it moved forward finally from the underbrush, allowed Byron to scratch its muzzle. It was an Indian dog, Byron realized, and must have belonged to a party that hunted these woods. He would do some hunting with the new gun, and take good care of the dog and himself. Life had begun to look a good deal better in the last hour.

But then, as he sat with the dog's head against his knee, he heard the men who advanced toward the hut. There were five of them; he recognized their voices. They were men suspected of cannabalism and were among the toughest in the crew. He got up quickly and loaded the gun.

The men stopped when he told them to halt. They told him that they did not want any trouble. What they were here for was the dog. They had seen it out in the woods this afternoon, and they were very hungry. Byron cocked the gun. His dog was not to be taken, he said. The men shrugged. If he fired the gun, they warned him, only one of them would be hurt, and the others would spend a long time in killing him. They would flog him first.

Byron lowered the gun. He turned his head aside. The dog tried to run, but the men were faster. It gave a couple of yelps and was still. Then a fire was started, and the meat put on a green wood spit to roast.

Byron moved over to the fire finally, and sat down, accepted a share of the meat. After all, he had done his best to save the dog. Some days ago, when the Indians had been here, Captain Cheap dealt with them for dog meat, offered bale goods for it. The lives of men were more important.

But hunger was what made him eat, Byron knew. It was the same sort of unreasoning hunger that would bring a man to cannibalism. That would be next for him unless he watched himself. He lay sleepless in the lean-to during the night, rose at dawn to go hunting. He would bring back food, he promised himself.

He waded through the sedge of the two big lagoons, stayed there for several days, and the best he could do was a scrawny goose, and a bird that flew so fast he called it a racehorse. The men at the camp looked bleakly at what he brought in, and spoke about the sheep and the dogs Captain Cheap had just bought. Those had been supplied by a party of Indians in exchange for trade goods. The Indians had not said when they would be back, and the sheep and dog combination meant only a single meal for all hands.

Byron kept on with the hunting. He worked inward

from the beach day after day, but the best he could find was a few woodcock and some humming birds so small they were almost inedible. But then, inevitably, he was embroiled in the bitter factionalism that was causing great trouble among the survivors.

Captain Cheap had shot and killed without much real provocation a midshipman named Cozens. For this, hatred of him had intensified, and a number of the warrant officers and seamen wished to get away from his command as soon as possible. The longboat from *Wager* had been hauled onto the beach, repaired and enlarged by the carpenter. She became a small two-mast schooner named *Speedwell*. It was the intention of the faction that opposed Captain Cheap to sail around Cape Horn and up the South Atlantic coast to Buenos Aires.

The gunner, John Bulkley, led the opposition to the captain. He greatly disliked Cheap, ignored Cheap's attempts to maintain authority. He was an excellent navigator, and had served as a watch officer aboard *Wager*. A large number of the survivors, 81 men all told, were willing to sail with him and take their chances rounding Cape Horn. They held, in addition to the rebuilt longboat, the cutter and another boat, and on October 13, 1741, they shoved off from the miserable beach and headed out to sea.

John Byron went with the strange little flotilla. He was awed by Bulkley's display of ability, and like all of the other men, so homesick, desperate, and starved that any plan to reach home made good sense. But the craft were badly overloaded. There was no discipline unless Bulkley exerted it. The first day's sail was short, and the men camped ashore. Byron took the opportunity to go back along the beach to the original camp. He had decided if he ever got home, he did not want the charge of desertion brought against him.

Captain Cheap said that he was almost ready to leave and

proceed up the Pacific coast and meet with Anson. The commodore should still be at the west coast rendezvous, waiting for *Wager's* arrival. But Cheap asked the men for patience. He said that the weather was very rough outside. Small craft could not survive in it

The men listened and shook their heads. A chance must be taken, they said. All that they had left to eat here was a weed called slaugh. Yes, and a little wild celery. Mixed with tallow and flour, and boiled, the best it did for a man was to give him a severe dose of dysentery.

A number of the men sagged to their knees with weakness while they talked with Cheap. He persisted, though, and told the strongest to come with him to the summit of the steep promontory they called Mount Misery. He pointed to seaward, where the wave crests broke in storm-driven fury. The boats would do poorly in that, Byron knew. Still, there was a chance. To stay here meant slow starvation or insanity. This was December 15, with the dark, awful days of deep winter ahead.

Captain Cheap listened while Byron spoke. His stubborn attitude had been greatly shaken by the departure of the group Bulkley led. He discussed quietly with Byron and some of the others what they should do. Then he said that he was fully ready to leave, make an attempt at the west coast passage. The men's hostility disappeared. They walked side by side with the captain to the beach, asking him how he thought the party should be divided into boat crews.

Cheap had regained the power of command. He ordered Byron to take the helm in the barge. He would sail with Byron, and the rest of the complement in that boat was formed by the surgeon, Mr. Elliot, and nine men. Lieutenant Hamilton and one of the lieutenants, Mr. Campbell, were assigned to the yawl with six men.

The party did not delay. The yawl followed the barge and Byron steered past the wreck straight through the center of the reef entrance for the open sea. He looked back when outside the reef, but only to take a bearing on Mount Misery. Then he faced the rough-pitching offshore combers. The men in these two boats, he told himself, were the last survivors of *Wager's* company, and very probably most of them would never make it back alive to England.

Night caught the boats close to a lee shore and with the wind against them. They were driven steadily to leeward. But there was a small opening in the reef and Byron put the barge through it, standing upright so that he could see, a man hanging to each of his legs to keep him from going overboard. The yawl was already inside the shelter of the lagoon, rode at anchor in the calm water.

The two boats stayed together after that and worked northward along the rocky coast where almost continuously the great westerlies smashed. Wilderness lay inland, then the snow-covered mountains, and the men knew that they must stay on the sea. But food was scarce; hunger never left them. They ate the soles of their boots, and limpets, mussels, seaweed, anything they could scrape from the rocks.

Captain Cheap was reasonably certain of Christmas Day, but the men lacked the energy to care. When Lieutenant Hamilton found a sea lion on the beach two musket balls were fired into the big beast. Hamilton leaped at it in absolute desperation and rammed a bayonet down the wide-gaping throat. The sea lion closed his jaws over the blade, broke it, swerved past Hamilton and into the sea.

Their luck remained bad. The yawl was lost when hurled against huge boulders alongshore. Four men must be left from her complement, Captain Cheap said. He named them, and they stood aside. Muskets and ammunition were handed to the four, and a frying pan, flint, and steel.

Captain Cheap nodded to Byron; he took the tiller of the barge while the rest crowded aboard. The men on the beach, all of them weak and unfit, cheered once Byron held the barge safely offshore. They waved their hats and shouted, "God save the King!" It would not be long, Byron knew, before they were dead in this wasteland.

Captain Cheap's objective was Chiloe Island. It lay in latitude 42°40′ South, and the southernmost Spanish settlement was on it. Byron began to believe that Chiloe was something that the captain had imagined. Cheap insisted that they reverse their course and go back to their original camp site on the bay where *Wager* had been wrecked. They must find a pilot from among the Indians, Cheap said, otherwise they would never make headway along the coast.

Some of the Indians with whom they had previously traded finally came back to the island. Several spoke a rough kind of Spanish. Their chief, a man named Martin, produced as a sign of his authority a stick with a silver head. He said he would serve as pilot.

Byron's hope greatly increased. He accepted the dangerously unwieldy load of fifteen men for the barge. The party started north again, the others following the barge in two Indian canoes.

It was terrific labor to row the barge. Byron took an oar, and sat on a thwart near John Bosman, the strongest man aboard. Bosman hauled until he reeled, and his breathing became harsh and very fast. Byron turned. He saw that Bosman had slipped from the thwart onto the floorboard.

Captain Cheap leaned down and told Bosman to rest easy. But he refused to feed the sailor, although Cheap had in his pocket a big piece of seal meat. Bosman was dying of hunger, Byron knew. He took from his jumper pocket five

Left: Statue of Alexander Selkirk at Largo.

Below: Cottage where Selkirk was born, and his sea chest with the cup that he used standing on it.

WILLEM
BARENTS

Left: Willem Barents and a drawing of one of his experiences in the Arctic titled, "How a frightful, cruel, big bear tare to pieces two of our companions."

Right: William Dampier and (*below*) John Byron.

Right: Herman Melville.

Below: Alfred R. Wallace, 1848 and Alfred R. Wallace, 1869.

or six dried shellfish, food that he had been saving for a final emergency. He gave them to Bosman. The sailor swallowed them, and blinked, and died.

Bosman hunched on the floorboard. Water slopped from beneath it and soaked his long hair. His body was pushed by the men as they shifted their feet to take a new grip on an oar, but they did not look down. Death was too commonplace for all of them, Byron thought. Even Bosman, who had pulled twice his weight in the boat, once dead, was almost wholly forgotten.

The husky young surgeon, Elliot, died a few days after Bosman. There was little sense in keeping dates, Byron thought. Every hour of this was misery. They had suffered the loss of the yawl and her four good men, and then what seemed like an endless succession of deaths.

Now, Captain Cheap said, this was finally Chiloe Island. Byron doubted him. He moved in a haze of despair. His last treasured possession, the fowling piece from *Wager*, was gone. He had given it at Captain Cheap's advice to the *cacique* who had guided them here. Next, Byron thought, he would be asked to offer a hand, or an arm.

But Indians who were warmly dressed and friendly came to welcome them. They were offered sheepskin ponchos to wear and taken to the town of Castro, fed, and given complete European clothing. A Jesuit priest who carried a bottle of brandy arrived to question them. He gathered up their rings and sea-ruined watches, conducted them to the nearby town of Chaco. They would stay in Chaco for some time, the priest advised them, and must be patient.

John Byron was perfectly willing to stay quiet. He slept through most of the days and nights of their easy captivity, learned a little Spanish from the guards, and dreamed of home. Then, in January of the winter 1742–3, the government ship made her call at the island. The Englishmen were marched from the jail where they had been held and put aboard her for Valparaiso.

Byron was curious about Valparaiso and tried to consider the future, and to disregard the past that brought him nightmares. Still, he could not forget that of out of *Wager's* original company there were only four of them left here— Captain Cheap, Lieutenant Hamilton, Mr. Campbell, and himself. Exactly how that had happened, he would never know.

The four, surprisingly well-received for men who had come to the Spanish colonies with the announced purpose of piracy, were sent on to Santiago from Valparaiso. The way was eased for them in Santiago by the presence of a Scottish doctor who had been in South America for a long time. He was known as Don Patricio Gedd, and he was unstinting in his friendship for the prisoners.

It took the Spanish authorities two years before a disposition was made of their case. Meantime, they were held in an almost casual form of custody. Captain Cheap was paid six *reales* a day for his subsistence, and the rest four *reales* a day. John Byron was able to make out quite well on his allotment, and as his health returned and the nightmares lessened, he became keenly interested in various aspects of local life.

His major concern was with the Chilean belles. He found them very beguiling. Their evening parade around the plaza, accompanied by their *duennas* and regarded by practically the entire male population of the city, made a lasting impression upon him. He described them years later in clear detail.

They walked with small, slippered feet over the cobblestones. Their long black hair was decked with flowers, the hair worn in four plaits. The shirtwaists inside the "little, tight waistcoats" were made of filmy lace. "Petticoats," he noticed, "open before and lap over, and have commonly three rows of very rich lace of gold or silver." Mantles and veils were worn, and silk stockings. Their embroidered garters were deliberately shown.

Byron remembered that the *señoritas* had "fine, sparkling eyes, ready wit, a great deal of good nature, and a strong disposition to gallantry." His next bit of description was about the drinking of *maté*, to which he gave much less space. That, he wrote, was drunk out of a silver bowl, through a straw.

Mr. Campbell left the group during their time in Valparaiso. He had been in long conversations with some of the clergy, changed his faith, and became a Catholic. So there were only three of them to go aboard the French ship *Lys* in December, 1774, with the knowledge that at last they were headed home. *Lys* was a St. Malo ship of 420 tons, a crew of fifty, and well-found. She carried fifteen guns, and after she had cleared Cape Horn in a snow gale Byron had great confidence in her.

She put into Cape François in north Haiti to make up convoy for home under escort of French Navy frigates. It was a safe and healthy passage, and on October 31, 1774, she reached Brest. The three Englishmen were sent ashore and told to make the rest of their way home any way they wished.

Captain Cheap made a deal with the master of a Dutch dragger, but the Dutchman cheated them out of their money, refused to take them across the Channel. Then, though, a British man-of-war came alongside the Dutchman when the trio's signals were understood. A boarding party was sent over from the man-of-war, and Cheap, Hamilton, and Byron were taken off the dragger. Royal Navy courtesy was extended further, and a navy cutter was put at their disposal which carried them to Dover.

The three survivors rented horses and started for London. It was too much of a ride, though, for Captain Cheap. He was about to collapse as they entered Canterbury. He and Hamilton decided to pool their money and take a post-chaise for the rest of the journey. Byron was to keep on riding his hired mount.

There in Canterbury, the shipmates said good-bye, and shook hands. Byron got up into the saddle and banged his heels against the horse. He had very little money left, and much less than enough to pay for the tolls along the road.

He galloped through all of the toll-booth stations along the turnpikes. He allowed the horse and himself small mercy, did not stop for food or water. When he came into London, he left the exhausted, lathered beast at an inn and took a hackney coach to the home of friends in Marleborough Street. But the house was closed, and he lacked the money to pay the coach driver.

He remembered a linen draper who owned a shop in the same street. He asked the draper if he remembered him, John Byron, and when the man said yes, borrowed the hackney fare from him. The draper was of further help. He told Byron that his sister had married Lord Carlisle and now lived in Soho Square.

Byron walked to his sister's home, and was almost turned away at the front door by the porter. His clothing was a weird mixture of Spanish and French, his knee-high boots spattered with turnpike mud. But his sister heard and recognized his voice, ran to greet him on the doorstep.

He had been away from England for more than five years. It was impossible for him to adjust at first to the existence of Lord and Lady Carlisle in Soho Square. Then news of the rest of Captain Anson's expedition was released by the Admiralty, and Byron began to understand that his suffering was very little in comparison to what had happened to the men in the other ships.

Just one of the seven ships in the original squadron returned to England. She carried, though, the immense loot taken at sea from the Manila galleon in a fierce battle. Byron, as a member of the expedition, would get his share of that. It was nearly time, he told himself, to seek out people he knew in the Admiralty, find another ship, and go back to sea.

🚢 *The need was very great. A new route must be found to Cathay and the Spice Islands. The future of the Netherlands depended on her sea trade, and the Spaniards in this last decade of the sixteenth century kept Dutch ships from entering the Pacific. So a search was to be made for the Northeast Passage, up into the ice wastes of the Arctic Sea.*

It was a region that very few men knew, and their information was not complete. Willem Barents was one who had cruised there several times. He was willing to serve as chief pilot for the expedition although he had already decided to retire from the sea, never again undertake the ordeal of the Arctic.

WILLEM BARENTS

*B*ARENTS came from the island of Ter Schelling, in the province of Friesland. He had been seagoing since he was a boy, and started as a fisherman. But his self-education was good. He wrote well in High Dutch, was an extraordinarily accomplished navigator, and held a thorough understanding of astronomy. When the Northeast Passage expedition was formed by Amsterdam merchants in 1594, he was a city burgher, and sufficiently prosperous to remain ashore the rest of his life.

Dutch maritime pride was extremely keen, though, and Barents was first consulted about the proposed Arctic voyage, then asked to take part. Amsterdam had become one of the principal ports of Europe, and her shipowners, merchants, and scholars worked together on many projects. Her cosmog-

raphers were the best in the Occident, and were in possession of rare and very valuable geographical knowledge.

The accounts of previous voyages to the Arctic had been
closely studied by them. They knew the details of Olivier
Brunel's penetration of the region. Brunel, a Dutch shipmaster, had gone first to the Kola Inlet, near the site of
present-day Murmansk. He left his ship there in charge of the
mate and went overland to the eastward, looking for a route
to Cathay. He entered Samoyed territory in Siberia, crossed
the Petchora River and, finally, the famous Ob River. Help
was given him by Russian merchants, and on his way back he
was able to set up a trading post at Archangel on the White
Sea, where English traders of the Muscovy Company were
already established.

Brunel returned safely to the Netherlands, and in 1584
made another Arctic voyage. The ship he sailed was owned
by the city of Enkhuizen, and his express purpose was "to
reach the far-off Empire of Cathay." Ice stopped him in the
high latitudes, but he was able to take aboard a cargo of furs,
mountain crystal, and Muscovy glass that would bring great
profit. Then the ship grounded in the shallows of the Petchora River mouth, broke up, and became a total loss.
Brunel's discouragement was so intense that he never went
back to the Netherlands, took service instead with the king of
Denmark.

English navigators had been busy in the forbidding
northern waters before Brunel met misfortune. Arthur Pet
and Charles Jackman conducted a successful Arctic voyage in
1580, and a translation of their account was given to Barents.
He studied it carefully and also a number of other books,
documents, and charts turned over to him by Gerhardus
Mercator, the famous cartographer, and Peter Plancius, who

was Barents' personal mentor and in his own right a master of geography and astronomy.

The key volume in regard to the Northeast Passage exploration was a thin, parchment-covered book of octavo size. It was *The History or Description of the Great Empire of China*. This had been written first in Spanish by Juan Gonzales de Mendosa, a monk of the St. Augustin order, then translated into Italian. The Dutch translation was done by "Corn. Taemz, and printed for Cornelius Claez, book-seller, living at the Gilt Bible in North Street, Hoorn, by Jacob de M——*, printer, in the town of Alkmaar."

The copy that Barents took to the Arctic with him was well-used, and he had given it hard scrutiny while still in Amsterdam. He had in addition various books and prints supplied for trading purposes in China. His navigation equipment was extensive. It contained an astrolabe, world globes, a pelorus, and several kinds of dummy compasses with wooden frames and surfaces with brass needles.

But he lacked Mercator's chart projections which would have been of great help in his course-plotting work in the difficult northern latitudes. The best charts available to him were of ordinary projections, and he was further hindered by a peculiar device that had been invented by Peter Plancius. The astronomer was responsible for the theory that there were eight meridians, under four of which there was no magnetic variation, and under the other four a maximum amount was to be found. His answer to the problem was a semicircular copper plate, the case curved so as to form parallels across the surface, and with a small, movable set screw in the middle.

It is quite doubtful that the Plancius invention was ever

---

* This name can no longer be deciphered in the copy available.

of assistance to Barents while he was trying to establish his ship's position in the Arctic. There was much more value in the theory that Plancius advanced about the direction to be taken for the Northeast Passage attempt. He firmly believed that ships should drive as far north as the ice permitted, then head due east.

But men who had been in the Arctic shipping trade for years believed otherwise. Balthazar Moucheron, a merchant from the town of Middleburg, was a major member of this group. Moucheron was one of the first Hollanders to trade in North Russia, and he and his veteran shipmasters were convinced that another, more southerly route was the best. This would be between the long-reaching island of Novaya Zemlya and the body of the continent itself, with the ships holding as close as possible to Siberia until they could enter the Pacific and set courses for China and India.

The expedition which Barents joined was small. There were three *vlyboots*, ships of about 100 tons each, owned by Moucheron and specially equipped for a voyage that might take them to China. They were strongly built, armed with light cannon, muskets, pikes, and halberds, and stocked with enough provisions for eight months at sea. One vessel was *Swan*, under command of Cornelis Cornelizoon Nai, a burgher of Enkhuizen who had for some years been pilot or master of merchant vessels in the North Russian trade. The second ship was named *Mercury* and her captain was Brant Tetgales.

Moucheron was a principal backer and sent along a pair of interpreters. Francis de la Dale, a relative of his with several years of trading experience in Russia, was assigned to *Swan*. A Slavonian named Christophel Splinder, who had studied at the University of Leyden, also went in *Swan*.

Barents was given command of the third ship, similar in almost every way to the others and, curiously, carrying the same name as Tetgales' vessel, *Mercury*. He took aboard for coastal work in shoal waters a fishing smack from Ter Schelling. He was both chief pilot and shipmaster. Neither he nor the men who would sail the smack seemed to consider Arctic conditions too severe for a craft of her size.

The fleet left June 5, 1594, from Huysdunen, off the island of Texel. A meeting of the captains had been held and Nai appointed commodore. It was agreed that the ships would keep together as much as possible, but meet again at Kildin, on the Lapland coast, if they separated. All of them reached the rendezvous on June 23, afterward stayed at the anchor, repaired ship, and gave the crews a chance to rest. Then, on June 29, they made sail. The understanding was that home-ward-bound they would put in here again at Kildin, wait for one another until the end of September.

Barents kept an independent course from the Lapland coast. He was about to test Plancius' theory of the far northerly route. Nai and Tetgales stayed together in the other two ships and headed for Vaigats Island, farther to the southward.

There was no ice in these waters, but a great deal of fog. Here the last of the Gulf Stream, the current called the Atlantic Drift, weakened and disappeared. Still, this was the season of high Arctic summer, and the sun hung red in the southern sky long enough to give Barents the observations he needed.

He made a landfall on Novaya Zemlya on July 4, established his latitude as 73°25′ North. He called the low, somber point of land he used Langenes, and stayed to seaward from it, kept on north along the coast. He passed Cape Nassau on July 10 and held on with his northing. He had not yet encountered ice, and told himself that perhaps off to the eastward, in another day or so, he would find the entrance to the passage.

But, during the short, gray hours of night on July 13, immense quantities of ice came down upon the ship. She groaned from the concussion, and her beams worked. Her deck planks heaved, buckling. The high-steeved bowsprit was almost smashed by floes. Barents walked the slanted poop deck and told the steersman to make good the present course. He was not yet ready to give up fighting the ice.

He changed his mind some hours later. Ice higher than the mainmast was butting out of the mist wraiths at *Mercury*. The men Barents had chosen for crew were intrepid, and fatalistic. But to be crushed to death was senseless and would prove nothing.

Barents gestured to the mate. The mate happily shouted the order, "Stand by to wear ship!" *Mercury* wore around with great creaking and thrashing of gear, the sails stiff with frozen fog.

She was driven back close to the land at Cape Nassau. Her hull was badly ice-chafed and battered. The crew was so weary that sometimes it took both watches to tack ship. But Barents was determined to try again for an entrance to the passage. He steered to the northward on July 19, and at the end of the month had raised the bleak, rocky Islands of Orange group.

Then his crew let him know, quietly, that they would not sail any farther north. It was a physical impossibility for them, Barents realized. Encumbered by layers of heavy clothing, thigh-high leather seaboots, and two or three pairs of mittens, and forced to haul and handle gear clogged with ice while working on slippery decks, they had come to the end of endurance.

They had been twenty-five days from Cape Nassau to this group of islands. Barents had tacked ship 81 times, and sailed according to his calculation 1,546 miles in ice. North of Cape Nassau alone, he had pushed *Mercury* 600 miles. Now he was finally ready to head the ship for home.

The mate was waiting, and the men, too, and when he gave the change of course to due south, there was relieved, rapid laughter. Hauling at the braces and the sheets, the watch started to sing a chantey. Barents murmured a few of the words into his beard. He was in his late fifties, but still young enough to be pleased that a ship was homeward-bound.

They met the other two ships a few days later. Both of the vessels were seaworthy, although their hulls showed wear from contact with ice, and the crews were gaunt, the men almost hysterically eager to get home. Nai and Tetgales said that, sailing in each other's company, the pair of ships had gone through the Yugorsky Shar. This was the strait between Novaya Zemlya and the northerly coast of the continent which Arthur Pet, the English navigator, had discovered.

Barents knew of its existence. But he was given to doubt the captains' statement about sailing more than 200 miles east of the strait. Nai and Tetgales insisted that their vessels had reached the longitude of the Ob River, near Cape Tabin. It was the farthest point in Russia, the shipmasters said, and from it "the coast trended to the southeast, towards the kingdom of Cathay."

There was a great celebration by the crews of the three ships and several toasts were drunk to their reunion. Then they continued the homeward course. They were greeted as heroes in the Netherlands. The reports made by Nai and Tetgales about their passage through Pet Strait aroused immense interest and it was decided to send a fleet of ships to the Arctic the following year.

Seven ships were dispatched by order of the States General on July 2, 1595, with an admiral in command and Willem Barents as pilot major. Barents sailed aboard a new

200-ton war pinnace named *Winthont* with some of his former crew. But tremendous amounts of ice were found off the coast of Novaya Zemlya and the fleet was forced to turn back. The voyage was a complete failure.

It was the decision of the States General that another voyage should not be given government support. But the authorities said that they would certainly award a generous sum to whoever discovered the Northeast Passage.

Barents was readily recruited for the third voyage. The Northeast Passage dream still claimed him. He sailed as chief pilot in a ship commanded by Jacob van Heemskerck. The other man was young, ambitious, and from a wealthy family of Amsterdam merchants who had invested in the voyage. Barents was perfectly willing to let Van Heemskerck take the responsibility of command; he had become a bit too old for that, and realized that in any emergency the younger man would listen to him. The second ship was commanded by Jan Cornelizoon Ryp, a shipmaster with considerable experience in the Arctic.

The theory held by Peter Plancius was to be tested again, and in the early spring of 1596 the pair of ships made the attempt to find the passage. They were far inside the Arctic Circle on June 9 when they closed with a small and steep island. Barents established the latitude as 74°30′ North, and a landing party met and killed on the beach a huge white bear. So the place was called Bear Island, marked as such on the ships' charts.

Cruising further north, the ships met extreme storm conditions and a huge quantity of ice. Barents and Ryp, the captain of the other ship, got into a dispute about what courses should be steered, and Ryp went off on his own. Barents still drove for the northernmost part of Novaya Zemlya, trying to clear it and stand past it to the eastward.

He was forced back, with the ship in great peril. When he established his approximate position as 77°45′ North, the sky was so overcast that he could not make an accurate observation. He was lucky to maintain a course along the western shore of Novaya Zemlya, and on August 26 he knew that very probably it would soon be necessary to abandon the ship. Ice might crush her at any time, and the winter must be passed here on the island.

The idea of wintering in the Arctic was not new, and often was used by Siberian hunters. This crew had been picked as much as possible from unmarried men, "that they might not be dissuaded, by means of their wives and children, to leave off the voyage." But it had never been done before by Europeans, and there was a considerable chance of scurvy due to a limited diet and lack of exercise during the long months of confinement because of the severity of the weather.

Van Heemskerck agreed with Barents about the abandonment of the ship. Huge, rough chunks of ice, forced by the pressure of solid fields far beyond, smashed against the hull, pushed the ship almost bodily up out of the water. The men hurried to get what they needed from her before she careened and they were drowned or crushed to death.

There was a strong wind from the Northeast on September 9, and the ship was shoved fully up onto the ice. Strakes around her rudder began to go while the men were in her main hold hauling out food supplies. They deserted the hold and spent the night hours on deck. There was still no shelter for them ashore, and two huge white bears moved close to shipside. Barents told the trumpeter to sound his instrument to drive the bears away, and muskets were fired. The bears retreated but had not been wounded. Barents and Van Heemskerck talked apart from the crew; the shore structure must be started right away despite the danger from the bears. The ship was no longer safe.

A party led by Van Heemskerck found along the beach an immense tangle of timber which the men believed had been seaborne from the mainland. The carpenter and his mate started measuring various logs for uprights, roof beams, and flooring after a site for the house had been chosen two miles inland from where the ship lay. The house was to be forty feet long and thirty feet wide, built of fir planks nailed to oak frames. Wooden bunks in the form of cubicles were built around the walls, an iron ship's stove installed in the middle of the floor, a barrel set over it in the roof to serve as chimney.

The men worked very hard. Loads of prepared timber were hauled twice a day from the beach to the house site. This was now late September, and the weather was colder every day. Rough wooden sleds were used for the loads, and the men trudged head down, the hauling ropes over their shoulders, straining, stumbling, sometimes falling on a slick patch of ice or packed snow.

But one man in each sled group was spared to guard the others against bears. He carried a musket, and walked on ahead, kept a sharp lookout. The bears were a constant menace, and some that had been killed measured as much as fourteen feet in length. One, a female, had been found with her head in a beef tub set partly submerged on the beach so that the meat would pickle. She was killed quite easily by a marksman, disemboweled, and her carcass propped up and left to freeze. The crew hoped to take it in that condition back to Amsterdam for exhibit.

Then, on October 10, a man started from the ship to join a work party and was almost caught. He sprinted back toward the ship yelling, "A bear, a bear!" The men aboard were all below to keep warm, and did not hear him. He was saved by the frozen bear; the live beast would not go past it, and the sailor scrambled up the ship's ladder to safety.

Two men and a boy were attacked a few days later while at work prying planks from the hull of the ship. A huge bear jumped aboard, and red-eyed, deeply growling, came along the deck at them. The men leaped down into the hold and tried to hide themselves among the rock ballast. The boy vaulted up into the fore rigging and went aloft as far as he could climb.

Other men aboard the ship threw chunks of wood at the bear and fired muskets. The bullets missed, but the wood chunks were on target and hurt. The bear retreated; the crew went back to work.

Willem Barents spent his time between the house and the ship, which was being rapidly stripped of whatever material could be used to finish the shore shelter. The ship's carpenter, a man Barents had known for years, overstrained his heart, and on September 23 fell suddenly dead. The ground was too hard-frozen for a grave to be dug, so the body was placed in a hillside gully, covered with gravel.

Barents felt saddened by the carpenter's death and was secretly worried about his own health. The season of sunlight was almost finished. For the next ten months they must live together, seventeen of them, in a single room, while outside the darkness and the cold pressed with awful power. It would become so cold that no man could live for more than a few minutes in the outer air.

He expressed some of his worry about the winter to Van Heemskerck, who brought Gerrit de Veer, the ship's surgeon, into the conversation. They decided that an enclosed porch should be built onto a side of the house to be used as a latrine and reduce the chance of sickness. De Veer arranged also to install a big wine cask near the center of the room and the stove. Water would be heated on the stove, and the men would take regular turns at steam baths in the cask. It was Barents' suggestion that a sail be stretched over the house roof and secured in place with loads of gravel. When the inevitable, heavy snow covered it, a protective canopy would be formed, containing the heat generated within the house.

Supplies of food and wine and beer were hauled into the house and stowed. Books, charts, a clock, candlesticks, a flute, navigating instruments, tools and weapons, and the men's personal gear were brought from the ship. Complete darkness came November 4, and the men found how terrible it was to live without sunlight.

Parties sent out from the house to gather wood reported that the bears had disappeared. It was the season of hibernation for the animals, Barents said. Now the enemy would be the white foxes. But the foxes could be trapped in nets; their flesh was edible, and the pelts would make warm hats.

The routine within the house gradually established itself and then changed very little. Men went out for wood, stayed no more than fifteen minutes, returned with big cold blisters on their faces and ears and their eyebrows frozen. The fox hunters made their nets of rope yarn, and were quite successful. They clubbed to death the beasts they caught. They came back, though, in the same part-frozen condition as the members of the wood parties.

Men took to their bunks and stayed there, close to coma, so depressed that they hardly moved. They got up when Van Heemskerck ordered them out on a wood-gathering detail; they took the steam bath in the cask when de Veer told them it was their turn. They ate their rations of salt fish, pickled beef, and sea biscuit, drank their share of wine and beer, went to the latrine, and that was about all.

Barents was seriously ill. A special bed had been built for

him and set right alongside the stove. He dozed a lot when the pain let him, then worked on his charts. The position here as he calculated it was 76°00′ North. The moon, observed through the door, was apparent for seven or eight days of the month.

When the wind was wrong, smoke was blown down the chimney and filled the house. Barents coughed until the pain made him want to scream. He watched the cook at the stove and finally laughed. The man had smoke tears rolling down his cheeks that left tracks through the smirch; he cursed in vile low Dutch and greatly regretted that he had ever left the herring boats.

Snow was brought from outside in buckets and heated for wash water. The surgeon insisted that the sheets be washed, and he supplied soap. The men obeyed, and took their turns at the buckets. But when the sheets were hung up, they froze on the side away from the stove. It was necessary to put them back over the steam above the buckets to get them fully dry.

Barents kept the hourglass going so that a record of their time spent here would not be lost. The cold had increased and stopped the ship's clock although weights had been added to the pendulum action. On December 11, the men's shoes froze. The shoes were thrown away as useless, cracked and sprung out of shape.

That loss made the men work. They fashioned out boots from fox pelts, put on three or four pairs of socks first.

The house was two miles from the sea, and yet from where they sat they could hear the ice crack.

The cold became worse December 12, and the men stayed in their bunks, did not even get up to heat stones against the stove to put between the blankets. Frost an inch thick covered their clothing, their blankets and sheets, and the walls of the house. Icicles formed in their beards from their breathing, and some men, in a fury of frustration, broke those off despite the acute pain that followed.

Sea coal had been found along the beach, and was put in the stove instead of wood. The fumes from it sickened them, though, and Barents said that they must burn only wood.

Men who still possessed the initiative took a trip to inspect the ship, carrying pine-knot torches. They reported that she was in bad shape. It was very possible that she would never sail again. Barents and Van Heemskerck said that an inspection made by torchlight proved little. They changed the conversation to the fox that had been snared and discovered solidly frozen. The carcass was thawed over the fire; the meat was prepared and eaten.

Then it was Christmas, and the men broke from their gloom for a bit. Gerrit de Veer, who kept the ship's journal, made a record of the occasion. He wrote:

"The 25 of December, being Christmas day, it was foul wether, with a north-west wind; and yet, though it was very foul wether, we heard the foxes run over our house, wherewith some of our men said it was an ill signe; and while we sate disputing why it should be an ill signe, some of our men made answere that it was an ill signe because we could not take them, to put them in the pot to rost them, for that had been a very good signe for us."

The men's morale improved after the dispute about signs was settled, and Barents was greatly relieved. Apathy brought on illness, he knew, and a man could easily relinquish himself to death, slip moment by moment toward it.

His pain had become so fierce that it was very difficult for him to think of anything except release. But he must hang on, he told himself; he must get back to Ter Schelling, his wife, and his family and friends before he died.

He dreamed often of his home in the hours when the pain was not too bad. He heard his wife singing as she started to prepare supper in the white-tiled kitchen. There was the scent of daffodils and crocuses through the open window beside him. Behind that was the salty rush of the North Sea wind. Windmills creaked. Dogs barked as they pulled carts along the cobbled street. Men whose voices he knew hauled their boats high on the beach for the night.

Barents counted once more the amount of time that must be spent here. It seemed endless when the pain tore at him. But January 5 was the Eve of Epiphany, he told himself, with daylight coming soon afterward.

The men celebrated Epiphany with much more enthusiasm than Christmas. They said that their stay here was almost finished, and they were about to go home. Van Heemskerck allowed special rations for the Three Kings ceremony, and each man was given a glass of wine. Flour that had been kept for cartridges was made into pancake batter, mixed with oil, and cooked on the stove. A "white bisket" apiece was served, and the men sopped them in their wine. They danced around the stove, singing, and the gunner was merrily crowned King of Novaya Zemlya.

Then hunters who were out fixing their fox traps on January 8 returned to say that they had seen signs of sunlight along the southern horizon. That brought about restlessness. Men stayed outdoors longer. They visited the ship to check her condition and found many tracks around her, and a foot more water in her hold.

Van Heemskerck and Gerrit de Veer and another man saw the sun simultaneously on January 24, verified the fact with each other. De Veer wrote in his journal:

"Wherewith we went speedily home again, to tell William Barents and the rest of our companions that joyfull newes. But William Barents, being a wise and well experienced pilot, would not believe it, esteeming it about fourteen daies too soone for the sunne to shin in that part of the world."

Barents was wrong, and the sun was actually visible. But a man who had lain sick for a long time took Barents' word, and on January 26 gave up hope and died. A fire was made to thaw the ground near the house and he was buried there. Barents felt a keen sense of remorse although Van Heemskerck told him that the man would have died soon under any circumstances.

The rest of the group were almost frantic with the return of sunlight. It was difficult for them to keep still. They wrestled, ran foot races, tossed a ball, played games that would give them enough exercise to escape scurvy. Then a marksman got a bear with a musket shot and they scraped a hundred pounds of grease from the carcass.

The grease allowed them to burn a lamp all night. It was called a good luck portent for the future. Men took turns perched up near the roof on a ladder, peering through the smoke vent barrel for ships that might arrive offshore. But no ship appeared, and the best the lookouts could report was that their own vessel had become a bears' den and was extremely dangerous.

When Van Heemskerck was absent from the house on May 9, the men came to Barents and asked the old pilot's advice. Wasn't it time to go? There was plenty of sunlight and to the southward the ice must be opening.

Barents was slow to answer. The pain prodded him terribly, and it was his nearly irresistible desire to tell the men, yes. But this was not yet the time, he realized. There was too much ice. If he gave his assent, Van Heemskerck would very probably agree, too, and the attempt would be made. Then they would all die, the strong, the weak, and himself, so ill that he could not walk or swim a stroke.

The men did not argue with him when he told them that the time was wrong. But they were more insistent when they came to him on May 11 and said that the wind was southwest and the water offshore was fairly open. Barents lay still until he could control his voice. He told them again that this was not yet the time, and to be patient.

His pain was evident to them, though, and they used it against him. They tried to make him change his mind and talk to Van Heemskerck, persuade the captain to leave. Some of the men told Barents that if the party left right away he could be treated by Russian surgeons on the mainland. There were drugs and medicines the Russians had which would help his condition. The treatment would enable him to get home to Ter Schelling.

Barents refused. He pushed the dream from his mind and said the men must wait for another few days. The men were impressed by the patience he showed. They agreed, and on May 16 he talked to Van Heemskerck.

The party left the island two weeks later.

There had been no meat for some days, and the men were clumsy with hunger when they began the necessary repairs on the two ships' boats that would carry them. Those were the yawl, and Barents' favorite smack, both in bad condition from the winter. But while the men worked on them a half-barrel of salt mackerel and some other provisions were found in the hold of the ship.

The ship herself had been shunted so high and far upon the ice that she could never be sailed again. Barents inspected her, towed on a sled, musketeers around him to keep away the bears. Then he told the men to take him back to the house.

He wrote a scroll with great care on June 13, made a record of the voyage. He requested that all of the men sign it, and thirteen signatures were attached. His was second under Van Heemskerck's, and the four who did not sign were either ill or unable to write. The scroll was put in a cartridge bandolier and hung in the chimney. If they were lost at sea while on the way home, there would be here some word for their people. He also wrote out a letter of sailing directions for each boat crew, in the event the craft might get separated or one of them be sunk by storm or ice.

That was the extent of his duties, and afterward he was given to the struggle against the agony.

The boats were ready. They had been hauled from where the ship lay to the water's edge over a road hacked across the ice. The supplies, some trade goods and the men's personal gear were aboard. Van Heemskerck designated the crews for each craft. Then, with the boats fully launched, Barents and another man who had been ill for a long time, Claes Adrianson, were brought down from the house.

Van Heemskerck gave the course that Barents had calculated. Sail was hoisted. Men bent to the oars, and with a west wind both craft got offshore and out of the Novaya Zemlya coastal ice field into the open sea. It was early in the morning when they left, and in clear sunlight. They could see the house for some distance, also the bears that stood guard on the wrecked ship.

The weather continued reasonably fair until June 17, when Gerrit de Veer reported: "In the morning, ice came so fast upon us that it made our haires stand upright upon our heades, it was so fearefull to behold."

They were confronted with the immediate loss of both boats. Men poised themselves, lines in hand, and leaped onto the slippery, lower shelves of the approaching floes. Then they hauled with all their strength and other men joined them, and the boats were dragged from the water upon the ice.

The sick men, wrapped in blankets and tenderly handled, were put down in the lee of the boats. A driftwood fire was started. Hunters went out and caught sea birds that were cleaned, cooked, and served. The boats were patched. With dawn, the party returned to the sea.

But the demands were too much for the strength Barents had left. He went into delirium on June 20 as the agony swept through his brain. He babbled about Ter Schelling, his wife, and the crocuses. Then he spoke of old shipmates whom he met again near the Montalbaans Tower on the waterfront in Amsterdam, and he thought he heard the chimes of South Church. He said that they reminded him of his iron clock, which rang the hour and half hour, and which had been left in the house on Novaya Zemlya. He recognized very briefly where he was, and he looked up into the faces of the men who knelt around him. "*Goede reis*," he told them. "Good voyage."

De Veer made a record of Barents' death. He entered in the journal, "The death of William Barents put us in no small discomfort, as being the chiefe guide and onely pilot on whom we reposed our selves under God."

The party was forced to climb up onto floe ice again on June 22 and drag the boats away from destruction. The men were starving, and when they put the boats back in the water and tried to steer the southwest course Barents had given them, they became separated. Musket signals brought them back together finally, numb from exposure and stooped with hunger.

Claes Adrianson died on that day, and five days later his nephew, John Franson, died. But the party kept moving. Van

Heemskerck had taken on added authority with Barents gone, and was a resolute commander. Hunters found bears on the floe ice, and one was shot, the meat consumed almost raw, and then duck eggs were discovered.

The men became very skillful at boat handling once they had regained their strength. During heavy weather on July 20 and while still off the coast of Novaya Zemlya, they ran among a huge school of walruses. Van Heemskerck estimated that there were as many as two hundred in the school, and he was afraid that they would crush the sides of the boats. But the boats worked through safely, and on July 27, near Sconce Point, lookouts reported a pair of Russian fishing boats to windward.

The Russians gave every possible assistance to the cast-aways. They showed Van Heemskerck the course to steer to reach the mainland, 120 miles away, and where they might next expect to meet other fishermen. The Hollanders still had with them some of the trade goods supplied by the owners for exchange in China. The stuff became useful along the Russian coast with various fishing boat crews.

Then, although the boats had been separated by bad weather, they came together again in the White Sea. The crews were able to rest, get back into shape and stand offshore for the run westward to the Kola Inlet. It was the central point for European shipping, and Van Heemskerck hoped to meet there a vessel that would take his people home.

The pair of boats entered the long, winding reaches of the Kola Inlet bow and bow. Men stared ashore and became speechless. Here were the first trees they had seen in more than a year, vast, fine stands of firs that reared close to a hundred feet from the ground. The air was aromatic. Birds sang; squirrels scampered after cones. And at the anchorage in the inlet was the ship that was commanded by Jan Corneliszoon Ryp. The same ship that had started the voyage with the vessel in which the survivors sailed.

Van Heemskerck boarded her and talked with Ryp. Arrangements were made to take the castaways home. Ryp's crew were generous hosts. They took good care of the men who had sailed almost 1,600 miles in open boats. But when the ship came into Amsterdam and tied up, de Veer wrote in the journal that the castaways went ashore "in the same clothes we ware in Novaya Zemlya, with our caps furd with white fox skins."

It might have been that the men were proud of their rough clothing and their strange caps and considered them to be badges of honor. They were ashore in Amsterdam near noon on November 1, 1597, met with the owners, were paid for the voyage, and went home.

Barents, in death, became famous. The sea in which he was given burial was named for him. Then, 275 years afterward, a Norwegian shipmaster, Elling Carlsen, went ashore on Novaya Zemlya. He found on November 12, 1871 the ruins of the house the castaways had built and occupied. Carlsen entered; he explored the place.

The roof had collapsed, and the entire structure was sheathed with ice. Still, he was able to take away many relics. Among them were a sword, and candlesticks, tankards, two compasses, the flute, five sea-chests, and Barents' clock. The iron hammer of the clock was poised to strike, and above it, hanging from the ruins of the smoke vent, was the bandolier that contained the record of the voyage, the last that Barents had ever written.

It was told so often that many of the details changed. But the basic story of El Dorado remained the same. Queen Elizabeth believed in it, according to the people who were close to her at court. Sir Walter Raleigh, out of favor with her and desperate to recoup his fortune, was willing to gamble his life and all he could borrow from his friends and family to discover it.

The story was that one of the Inca princes of Peru, a relative of the murdered king, Atahualpa, had fled from Spanish persecution. He went eastward from Peru, across the Andes. He took with him thousands of his people and an immense amount of treasure. Then he became emperor of what he chose to call Guiana.

His capital city was Manoa, on an inland sea that was 600 miles long. The territory he ruled reached from the Amazon to the upper Orinoco. All of the local Indian tribes accepted his authority, and brought him their gold and other treasure. A Spanish soldier who had been captured and held in Manoa swore as he was dying that he had spent seven months in the place. When he was free to leave the city, it took him thirty hours to walk from the center to the outer wall.

Spanish expeditions had tried for fifty years to get to Manoa. Englishmen were just as eager to make the attempt. They gave as an answer to criticism of some of the more fantastic claims, the history of the wealth seized in Mexico, in Cuzco, and Quito. Priests daubed with gold dust and using golden daggers upon their victims in orgiastic ceremonies might well exist. Similar rites had been witnessed by the Spanish conquerors in Mexico.

Raleigh read every account of Spanish exploration that he could acquire. He knew of the attempt made by Hernan Perez de Quesada to go from New Grenada through the jungle and along the precipitous rivers to Manoa. He had heard also of the expedition led recently by Antonio de Berreo. The Spanish officer had started from New Grenada with 700 horsemen, 1,000 oxen, and hundreds of Indian slaves. Berreo went down the Rio Negro to the Orinoco; disease and disaster took nearly all his people and, although he persisted for 1,500 miles, he never reached Guiana.

But, for his effort, King Philip II had made him Governor of the island of Trinidad, off the South American coast. Berreo claimed in the name of his king in April, 1593, the entire Orinoco region. Raleigh, informed of this, stalked restlessly through London, raising the last of the money he needed for the venture he proposed.

Raleigh was able to sail from Plymouth on February 6, 1595, in command of five ships and some small craft for river exploration. He had with him a number of the most distinguished officers in England; the lure of the voyage was very great. Wealth, honor, and advancement could be found at El Dorado, and the hazards were to be disregarded. Life itself had little value.

SPARRY and GOODWIN

THEY HAD come here in the night along the lightless river, and now, having deeply slept, they stared curiously about them. The Englishmen saw that this was the largest Indian village they had reached on the Orinoco. The huts were made of palm thatch, with the roofs sharp and high, and strange bits of carving over the doorways. There were more than twenty huts in regular rows back from the steep bank. The Indian dugout canoes were drawn up there, and below them, secured to stakes, the three English pulling boats.

The Englishmen left the huts where they had slept. They went into the street under the tremendous white blaze of the South American sunlight. A few of them could speak Spanish; they talked with a man who wore a jaguar-skin breechclout but carried a Spanish cutlass. He said the tribe called themselves Araucas. The village was known as Aromaia, and the chief of the tribe was Topiawari, who was 110 years old. Spaniards were the tribe's enemies. The man who spoke had been made a slave and then run away from a military post downriver.

The Englishmen were bareheaded and barefoot, their hair grown down to their shoulder blades since they had left the ships in the Gulf of Paria on the coast more than a month ago. Chiggers had infected and swollen their calloused feet. Twigs, gnats, mosquitoes, and flies were matted in their hair, and their cotton pants were mud-smeared, badly ripped. Still, the men strutted when they passed a hut where the almost naked Indian women crouched. They made bawdy jokes about the women's breasts and slapped each other on the back. But when they reached a hut that was bigger than the rest they were silent. It belonged to the chief, they recognized, and Raleigh and the other gentlemen were inside in conversation with him.

Goodwin went a few paces away from the other men. They still considered him to be a boy, he realized, and occasionally allowed him to act like this. None of them understood, of course, that he preferred to be alone, that all of his life until he had joined Raleigh's fleet and gone to sea, he had never been free from people. The Covent Garden slum where he was born, and the various mean and terrible places he stayed with his mother before her death, all seemed in memory to be crowded with people, and were filled with their sounds and smells and pressing, thrusting bodies.

For Goodwin the jungle was like escape from prison. And the worst part leading to it had been the passage outward-bound. If he had known in Plymouth there were going to be so many men crammed together in the dark foulness of the lower decks of the ship, he would have stayed ashore, hunger and all.

Goodwin stared keen-eyed at the chief's hut. Something was about to happen there. The bosun from *Lion's Whelp* had just stepped into the street. He told the men to form a single line and beckoned to Goodwin. A hundred men, Goodwin thought, picked from the fleet because of their brains and brawn. But they stood here like sheep in a village square on market day. They did not even ask why the bosun had told them to form the line.

Now, though, Sir Walter Raleigh stepped to the door of the hut and the men stood straight and touched their fore-locks in salute. Raleigh always received respect like that. When the going had been hard on the river and the men were so fatigued they could not lift the oars, Raleigh took his turn, mocked the other gentlemen until they joined him. His velvet and his lace were soiled; there were stains on his doublet, and one of his boots was ripped. But his sword was clean. He was freshly shaved, and his dark brown hair and little, pointed beard were combed. Goodwin felt a flicker of pride over the fact that he belonged to Raleigh's company.

The men entered the hut one by one. They halted beside a water cask that had been taken from the longboat and was used as a table. Captain George Gifford, second in command to Raleigh, stood there. His scrivener was bent over it, in front of him a list of the men who were assembled here.

Goodwin noticed while he waited that the chief, Topi-awari, sat in a corner, knees under his pendulous belly, the myopic eyes almost shut. But Topiawari drew busily upon the new clay pipe that Raleigh must have given him, and the smell of the Virginia tobacco was fragrant in the sweat-heavy air. Raleigh had been very careful to make friends, Goodwin realized. The chief was an important man and could send the company on the way to El Dorado.

That was the reason for the muster. Raleigh had to get back to the fleet. The ships were shorthanded, and the Spaniards in force nearby at Trinidad. There was no gold to take to England, or precious gems. Still, Raleigh had great hope in the various samples pried from the rock formations along the river banks, and he must report to the Queen and to the people who had raised the money for the expedition. He planned to return as soon as he could; meanwhile, he would leave men here in the country.

Captain Gifford's scrivener read the names from the list, and Gifford bluntly asked the question. Was the man willing to stay here and serve the cause of Her Majesty, and make himself wealthy? The answers were sometimes slow, Goodwin noticed, but all of the men refused. They had no liking for the jungle, the fever, the snakes thicker than a man's arm, the alligators that had eaten Sir Walter's servant, the jaguars that screamed like women in pain but killed with a swift, single leap from the bamboo brakes. They wanted home, the few ducats coming to them for pay, a night or so with a tavern bawd, then another ship.

It was Goodwin's turn, and the usual mistake was made. He told Captain Gifford, "No, sir. That's my name. Goodwin is all."

The bulky captain stood unsmiling. He looked at Raleigh, tall and straight in the narrow doorway. Raleigh gestured, and it was meant as an order for the captain. Goodwin understood.

Gifford asked him then, "Will you stay here, lad, till the ships come back next year?"

"Yes, sir," Goodwin said. He remembered to touch his forelock before he stepped aside.

There were not many more after him. All of them refused, and along toward the end Gifford was quite angry. He
told the men that Captain Caulfield, who commanded a vessel
in the fleet, and young Gilbert and Grenville, both Raleigh's
cousins, had volunteered to stay. The men said nothing in
reply. They just backed from the hut. Raleigh stopped Goodwin from joining them.

Goodwin understood then that the other who was to
stay here was the scrivener. His name was Francis Sparry, and
he was a couple of years older than Goodwin, a handsome and
strongly built young man. When he spoke it was not with
the broad West Country accent that most of the company
used. Raleigh liked to take in his ships men from his native
Devon, or from Cornwall. But Sparry talked in a clipped,
college-educated voice.

Sparry was a gentleman, Goodwin told himself. A very
ambitious gentleman. If not, why had he volunteered for
what all of the rest considered to be a miserable and dangerous task? Sparry stared across the hut at Goodwin, his glance
shrewdly calculating, and barely nodded. He turned afterward and asked Raleigh how soon the boats would leave for
the coast.

Before sundown, Raleigh said. He motioned to Goodwin
and brought him to stand beside Sparry. Then he told them
what their duties were. Sparry was to write a book about the
country. He was to explore it, try to reach a village on the
Guiana frontier, observe all that he could. Goodwin was to
learn the local Indian dialects, become a close friend of the
men in this tribe, hunt and fish with them. The chief's only
son was being taken to London by Raleigh, and the Spanish
were sure to resent the fact. Spanish patrols could be expected
in the village, and Goodwin must know how to take care of
himself.

Next year, the ships would return. Boats would come up from the coast. Sparry and Goodwin should be ready to join them, make sure to get word in advance from the Indians. Spanish pursuit was always possible.

Raleigh wished the pair good luck, and held out his hand. Francis Sparry took it and bowed so low that he almost touched it with his forehead. Somehow, that embarrassed Goodwin, and he only saluted Raleigh, and moved quickly from the hut.

He spent the rest of the afternoon with the sailors he had come to know in the ship. One gave him a knife, another a flint and steel. He would need them, they said. Then the men were called to the boats. They took their places. The trumpeter sounded; Raleigh drew his sword and waved the blade in a circle of light. The Indian dogs barked, following the two wherries and the longboat for some distance on the bank.

The Indians, Goodwin, and Sparry stood silent. It was Sparry who spoke first. He said that he had made arrangements to live in Topiawari's hut as a guest of the chief. Goodwin could stay any place he liked. Goodwin thought of the friendly Indian with the Spanish cutlass. He smiled happily at Sparry and went on alone along the street.

Sparry left the village a few weeks later, as soon as he had mastered some of the Indian dialect and could recruit a canoe crew. It was his intention, he told Goodwin, to go up the Orinoco to the Caroni, then ascend that river to the frontier of Guiana. He would collect material for the book Sir Walter had ordered him to write. And gather, Goodwin thought, a private fortune in gold and gems along the way if they were to be found.

But Goodwin said nothing except to wish Sparry well. He was content here. He learned more every day about the habits of the tribe and was profoundly pleased. His hope was to become a very skillful hunter.

He already had his own five-foot long blowgun and a quiver of arrows whose tips were touched with the deadly curare poison. His Indian friend, who bore the Spanish name of Juan, had shown him how to use the blowgun, but after that let him go into the jungle by himself.

Goodwin hunted often in the wide savannahs that stretched back from the river. They had been cleared originally by fires that lightning had started when large trees were struck. Some were several acres in extent, covered with yellow Guinea grass that grew waist-high and waved in the river breeze. It might also contain a waiting jaguar or a peccary, one of the fierce and long-tusked wild hogs even the jaguars feared.

Goodwin climbed up into the top branches of a tall silk-cotton tree, and from that vantage studied the jungle. He saw a jaguar stalking a careless anteater, and a spider monkey who hung half-asleep from a branch a boa constrictor could reach. Bees built their nests in the silk-cotton trees; he discovered how to raid the honeycomb without disturbing them. He spent hours just listening to the bird sounds, and sat so still that immense azure and lavender and amber-colored butterflies came to rest on his naked shoulder.

Then, with Juan's help, he learned about the river. They fished together, using bamboo spears. Turtle eggs were dug from the bank mud. Alligators, snapping and barking, were trapped in the shallows, flopped on their backs with a spear thrust, and easily killed.

Goodwin began to forget about England. He no longer counted the days since Raleigh's company had left for the coast or Sparry had gone upriver. His cotton pants were worn out, and he made a breechclout from the skin of the first jaguar he killed. Juan had a sister whose teeth were better and who was much cleaner than the girls of her age Goodwin knew in England. He gathered pineapples for her, and climbed the palms to shake down the coconuts which gave the Indians their beer and flour. Then, after Juan assented, Goodwin built a hut, moved into it with the girl.

Sparry came back to the village gaunt with fever and without treasure. He had been gone for more than seven months, he told Goodwin, and had reached the great falls on the upper Caroni River. It was his belief that if El Dorado existed, the place was much farther away in the interior of the continent. Indians he met on the Caroni told him conflicting stories, still none of them would admit they had ever seen Manoa or had been in the empire of Guiana.

Goodwin sat quietly and listened to Sparry, then asked the other man what he proposed to do next. Sparry stared at him in surprise. He wanted to get back to England, he said. He very much missed Canterbury, and all of his life there, also his family and a girl he had promised to marry. She came from a fine Kentish family, he said; her people had money.

Goodwin said that to get out of here meant going down the Orinoco to the coast. There was no other way. Men like themselves, no matter how much the Indians helped them, were certain to be caught by the Spaniards on the lower river. He had no fancy for a Spanish prison or a lifetime job chained to an oar aboard a galley.

Sparry shrugged. Let him think about a way around that, he said. He rose and for the first time took a full look at Goodwin's girl. Then he walked away without saying good-night.

Sparry stayed in the village for three months. He sat during the daytime in the doorway of the chief's hut and worked on the book. Goodwin was interested; Sparry seemed to use with great skill the quill pen, the brass inkpot, and the long sheets of parchment that Raleigh had left him. But Goodwin could not read, and he was aware that he shared very little in common with Sparry. He kept away from the man as much as possible.

It was Sparry, though, who brought Goodwin the news that there were Englishmen on the lower river. Sparry said that he had heard it from one of the Araucas who had served in his canoe crew. The Englishmen, according to Sparry, had come up the Orinoco within musket shot of the Spanish town of San Thomé, several days journey from here. The English party was commanded by Captain Lawrence Kemys, one of Raleigh's shipmasters during the voyage last year.

Goodwin was doubtful. He told Sparry that if Captain Kemys got as close to this village as San Thomé he would come and save them, make good the promise Raleigh had given. Sparry laughed. He said that Goodwin knew only a small amount about Sir Walter.

Wealth was what counted to Raleigh, not peoples' lives. Raleigh had left the company of settlers in Virginia to die, and in the same way they were being deserted here.

He and Goodwin were castaways, Sparry said. They no longer existed in Raleigh's calculations. The only thing to do was get out of here on their own as best they could. Goodwin answered that he was not sure and wanted to talk with Juan.

But Juan verified what Sparry said. He had contact with the Indians who were slaves of the Spanish at San Thomé. It was Captain Kemys who had approached San Thomé and left without firing a shot or trying to get past the place. There had been no attempt to reach them here.

Goodwin went and talked with Sparry outside the chief's hut. He was staying, he said. His wife—he no longer called her his girl—was pregnant. And if he fell into the hands of the Spanish, things would go very hard for him. He had no people at home to pay ransom, and no money of his own.

Sparry expressed regret. He did not like leaving Goodwin here alone among the savages. Still, he must return home. His book was finished and should be published in England to tell of the marvels of this country. Then there was his girl in Kent, and the fact that he was betrothed to her.

Goodwin understood. He shook hands with Sparry and wished him Godspeed home. Then he offered some smoked monkey meat, and some fish and fruit that would hold Sparry until the man reached San Thomé. The offer was accepted, and the next day at dawn, in a canoe he handled himself, Sparry started downriver.

Goodwin heard a week later of Sparry's safe arrival at San Thomé. He was in the custody of Captain Felipe de Santiago, commandant of the post there. He was to be sent on to Trinidad and then to Spain after ransom was paid. Goodwin was glad. Francis Sparry was the kind of man who belonged in England.

The years after Sparry's departure went unmarked by Goodwin. His only record of time was the change in seasons, and the growth of his sons and daughters. Topiawari died, and was replaced by Juan, and when the Spanish patrols entered the village, there was plenty of warning. Goodwin hid out in the jungle until the Spaniards were gone. Juan finally told a Spanish officer that Goodwin had been killed by a jaguar, and the soldiers did not return.

Goodwin lived in peace. His body thickened some as his sons grew up and took his place as a hunter. There was a little gray in his hair, and he realized that he had entered middle age. But he was not bothered by the fever. He took regularly the bitter drafts his wife made from the cinchona bark to combat it, and mosquitoes were just a nuisance during the hours he wished to spend fishing on the river.

Then, once more, there were rumors of English ships off the coast. This greatly disturbed Goodwin. He no longer considered himself an Englishman. If he held any loyalty, it was to his wife's people, and Juan regarded him as a sub-chief of the tribe. He had almost forgotten how to speak English, talked it only for the amusement of his youngest sons.

He was surprised and shocked the day the blunt-bowed wherry came in out of the river mist. It was wet, squally weather, and the craft was swung rapidly from the center of the stream. Goodwin stood at the top of the bank where the village canoes were kept. He was ready to go fishing, held his spear and his long, tapered paddle.

The armed men who jumped from the wherry were English, he saw. So, too, were all of them in the boat, except the Indian guide. Some of those aboard were wounded, and there were bullet holes in the hull planks.

Goodwin was told to drop the spear. Then the man who gave the order scrambled up the bank. He wore a steel casque, a gorget and corselet, and one of his long Cordovan boots was filled with blood from a leg wound. His pistol was silver-chased, his sword a magnificent weapon. Goodwin felt a sudden impulse to salute. Here was a second Walter Raleigh, returned across the vast gap of the years.

His thought seemed to be fully understood. "I'm Sir Walter's son," the tall and dark young man said, "and bear the same name. You'd be Goodwin. The Spaniards reported you as killed by tiger."

Goodwin explained, his English halting, and very slow. Juan and most of the other warriors had advanced from the

huts, and carried weapons, Goodwin saw. He told young
Raleigh that they thought the English meant to harm the
village.

Walter Raleigh said they had no such intention. What
they looked for here was gold. They sought the mine which
Captain Kemys claimed was on this stretch of the river and
had tried to find during the 1595 expedition.

The mine did not exist, Goodwin said. Goodwin spoke
hard-voiced, feeling anger. He wanted to know where Captain Kemys was, and why the captain failed to look for the
mine himself.

Kemys was down at San Thomé, where a skirmish was
about to be fought, Raleigh said. The captain was in command of the English shore force. Sir Walter Raleigh led the
expedition and was aboard ship off the coast. Sir Walter had
every hope that the gold mine would be found, and for that
reason had sent the force upriver.

Goodwin turned deliberately and translated what had
been said to Juan and the other warriors. The Englishmen
should put down their weapons, Juan told Goodwin. This
village did not belong to them, and the Araucas were not
their enemies.

Young Raleigh cursed when Goodwin translated back
to him. He put his pistol in his belt, though, and told the
sailors below on the bank to lower their weapons. The Indian
who had been the guide from San Thomé slipped out of the
wherry and showed his empty hands to Goodwin. He was
very sorry that he was here, he said, then disappeared into the
jungle.

Goodwin stared steadily at Raleigh. He said that the
Englishmen should get into their boat and go back down the
river. They were wasting their time. The gold mine which
Sir Walter wanted to find was no more real than El Dorado.

Those were stories which should be kept for ale-house talk in England.

The thin-faced young man blinked. His hands started to tremble, and he took the weight off his bad leg. Then he said, "We must get to San Thomé. The Spaniards were hard after our people there when we left. If the mine ——"

"There is no mine," Goodwin said. "So get out of here."

He was moving away when Walter Raleigh caught him by the arm. "We can't even find our own way back to San Thomé," he told Goodwin. "Help us."

"Why?" Goodwin said harshly.

"Because," Walter Raleigh said, "my father brought you here. He gave you this life. You owe him a debt."

Goodwin stood still. He looked out over the river and heard it and the jungle and the village sounds, as familiar to him as his own breathing. But the wounded men in the boat watched him, and he knew that several of them would die unless they were given care. They trusted him. He was Goodwin; he was an Englishman. If he failed them, the entire party would fall into the hands of the Spanish. There would be then a considerable amount of torture before death. The Spaniards were very jealous of their possession of this part of the country.

Goodwin spoke to Juan. He explained to the chief why he must go away with the Englishmen. This was owed, he said, and he did not know any other means to repay it. Juan should say good-bye to Goodwin's wife for him, and to his sons and daughters. He lacked the time. The Spaniards were already waiting down at San Thomé.

Juan did not speak. He handed Goodwin the Spanish cutlass, though, and when the wherry shoved off from the bank he and the warriors sent her clear into the stream. Goodwin sat beside young Walter Raleigh, took the tiller.

When the wherry was in the final reach above San Thomé and they could hear the musket shots, Goodwin talked with Raleigh. He asked Raleigh what year this was. It was 1617, Raleigh said. And, Goodwin wanted to know, when had Francis Sparry returned to England? In 1602, Raleigh said. The Spaniards had made the family pay a hugely increased ransom.

The English force was pinned down by Spanish musket fire at San Thomé. But when Walter Raleigh's people arrived, Captain Kemys decided that an attack should be made on the town. It seemed wholly logical to him that Goodwin was with the party, and he told Goodwin to take part in the attack.

Young Raleigh led the way from the landing place into the narrow, muddy street before the plaza. The Englishmen were short of ammunition, and they were armed with pikes. They were almost at the Spanish barricade when the heavy volley was fired. Raleigh was killed along with several others, and in the retreat it was hard to carry away their bodies.

Kemys was furious, although he had ordered the retreat. He told the Englishmen to set fire to the houses on the outskirts. There was a stiff breeze on the river. All of the wooden-built houses were ablaze as the English force left in their boats and crossed the stream.

Kemys spoke about making another attempt to find the gold mine. But Goodwin dissuaded him. Goodwin said there was no such mine, and that smoke from the fire would be seen by other Spanish garrisons. If Kemys wanted to get down the river alive and reach the fleet, this was the time.

There was some pursuit on the lower river, but Goodwin knew how to hide the boats in among reeds in the backwaters. The force came without further injury to the mouth of the river and the open sea. The oarsmen pulled hard with the ships in sight, and Goodwin looked up and saw that Sir Walter's ship was named *Destiny*.

He boarded her at Kemys' insistence, Kemys close beside him on the ladder. The reason for this, Goodwin realized, was that the captain wanted him to fill out his report when he talked to Sir Walter. It was too late for him to go back now, though; he had made his choice.

The cabin Sir Walter occupied was in the huge after-castle of the ship. There were bookshelves along the bulkheads, and pictures. Fine rugs were on the floor. The furniture was dark, and massive. Light came spangled through the colored glass of the after windows.

But Goodwin did not pay much attention to the cabin. The smells of the ship almost overcame him—smells of filth and sickness. He remembered the crew's quarters in the ship in which he had sailed from England, and these must be just as bad. He would share them on the return to England, far below the main deck, hammock slung against hammock, body butting body, while the rats chased over the men who slept, were sick, or dead.

Sir Walter came to the door of the cabin and vaguely greeted him. Goodwin touched his forelock in reply. He could do that much and no more. Sir Walter was stooped with the years. Great streaks of white were through the long hair and beard. The eyes were sunken within yellowish, puffed lids. But the clothing was magnificent, plum velvet and gilt lace, hundreds of small pearls sewn on the doublet, and more pearls and precious gems on the matching slippers.

Sir Walter stared at Captain Kemys. He asked about the trip upriver and wanted to know why his son was not here. Kemys made the report in a thick, slow voice. Some of the words he said clotted together and failed to form sense. Sweat was on his face. He could not meet Sir Walter's gaze.

Then Sir Walter began to curse him in a shrill and terrible voice. He told Kemys he would have the captain broken and imprisoned when the fleet reached England. There had been strict orders given by him to Kemys not to fight the Spanish at San Thomé, or burn the place. Nor should Walter Raleigh be dead. And the gold could have been found.

Kemys left the cabin while Raleigh still talked. He walked past the junior officers out on deck and went down a ladder. Goodwin started after him, but Sir Walter called him back. He had slumped into a wide, cushioned chair. His ring-set hands were gripped on his knees, and they twitched.

"Tell me of Guiana," Sir Walter said.

"It is a faraway place," Goodwin said. "No men have reached it yet from the outside." He kept on, reweaving the old legends, and aware that as long as he talked about El Dorado this man would listen.

Then Kemys was back. He held a letter that he tried to make Sir Walter accept. It was written to Lord Arundel of the Council, he said, and was in defense of his action at San Thomé. He wanted Sir Walter to forward it to London.

Sir Walter refused. Kemys stood speechless, and finally bowed, went from the cabin. Sir Walter spoke as if he sat alone and Goodwin did not stand within the doorway. This was the end, Sir Walter said. Now the Spaniards had trapped him, and for the blunder at San Thomé, when Spain and England were supposed to be at peace, he would lose his head.

A strange fascination kept Goodwin there. This was a man, he knew, who was supposed to be one of the greatest of his age. Sir Walter had been Queen Elizabeth's favorite for years, and a famous soldier, statesman, poet, historian, philosopher, chemist, admiral, and explorer. The boat crew had been talking about Sir Walter on the way here from San

Thomé. They said that nothing could harm him despite the Spanish plots. He was too smart, and knew how to stay out of trouble with King James. The man would never lose his head under the ax.

But Sir Walter sat bent in the chair, his hair around his face, his eyes shut. When he spoke, it was of his son. He did not look up as a junior officer came to report that Captain Kemys had just killed himself. Kemys had tried a pistol first and only broken a rib. There was a long knife in the cabin, though, and he had succeeded with that.

Darkness came over the ship and the sea. Lanterns were lit on deck. A servant entered quietly and set tapers in sconces around Sir Walter's cabin. Sir Walter looked up, haggard, in anguish. "So there is no El Dorado?" he asked Goodwin.

"That is right, Sir Walter," Goodwin said.

Sir Walter rose, and walking stiffly, went out on deck. He called to the senior officer. The fleet was to be ready to sail at dawn and proceed to England. The expedition was finished.

Goodwin heard the order and moved toward a ladder that would take him below to the halfdeck. But he looked back once more at Sir Walter. Light from the immense stern lanterns touched Sir Walter, brought a luster from the gems he wore. Goodwin realized that there was more wealth on Raleigh's slippers than he had seen in all of the jungle years.

Back in England, the part that Goodwin had played in the two expeditions was nearly forgotten. He disappeared; no further record was kept of him. But Raleigh had been quite correct in the prediction about himself. Sir Walter died under the headsman's ax for the mistakes made along the Orinoco.

During the 1840's, more than 4,000 men a year deserted American whaling ships and went ashore on various Polynesian islands.

There was a paramount reason for this drastic crew shrinkage. The masters and mates of many of the whalers wanted the men out of the ships and followed a deliberate design to make them castaways, with no hope of return aboard for the passage home.

Some of the men had proven themselves cowards while chasing whale, or were malingerers, or potential mutineers. Others could not stand the prospect of another year, perhaps more, aboard ship in the vast emptiness of the Southwest Pacific. They were enticed ashore by the beauty of the islands, the ease of life there, and the grace, fervor, and sexual freedom of the Polynesian women. A few men in every crew had contracted venereal disease, and their shipmates refused to stand watch for them and share the same cramped fo'c'sle. But the majority were driven ashore by the greed of ships' officers, so badly treated that only one choice remained, murder or desertion.

A man who had gone on the beach in the Marquesas could not claim his part of the payoff at the end of the voyage in New Bedford. It was wholly possible for a shipmaster, assisted by his mates, to falsify the logbook entries as to just when and why a man had left the ship. His gear could be sold in the next port, and his place taken by a Polynesian islander, often on a workaway basis. This was a common occurrence.

But Herman Melville was moved by quite different and almost wholly individual compulsion to leave the brig Acushnet. He had waited six years to reach this particular island. Now he was intensely eager to get ashore and desert.

HERMAN MELVILLE

ACUSHNET was a new ship when Melville joined her in December, 1840, in Fairhaven, across the bay from New Bedford. She was a Rochester-built brig of 350 tons, laid down in the sturdy Massachusetts whaler fashion to the careful specifications of her owners. Now, a year and a half later, having cruised both coasts of South America and the enormous Southwest Pacific reaches, she was dilapidated, and foul. Melville hated her.

His sensitive mind could not accept without violent dislike the brutality of her master, Captain Valentine Pease. Her record as a whaler was poor, and almost from the start of the voyage there had been trouble between Pease and his officers and the crew. The first and third mates left the ship at Paita, in Peru, and the first mate had fought bitterly with the "tyrannical captain." A man had run away at Roa-pua in the Marquesas, and others skipped the ship at Maui, hid out until she sailed.

Melville who was aboard her as an ordinary seaman had been fully willing to do his share of work while she had whale in sight, and actually took a fierce kind of delight from being exposed to danger. But the endless stupidity aboard ship, the reiterated punctuation of a brutal show of authority, threats, rope-end beatings, fist and boot blows corroded the final residue of his patience.

He stood on her main deck in Nukahiva harbor and looked ashore with a longing that made every detail memorable to him. He had just learned that there was no terminal date for the voyage; it might go on for three, four, five years. If the oil casks in the holds weren't filled, Captain Pease would keep her at sea, running back and forth across the Line, between the tropic latitudes and the Antarctic. Her only reason for being here was that she badly needed fresh water and provisions.

Melville was twenty-two. He was not prepared to spend any more time aboard *Acushnet*. He studied the shore and planned exactly how he would reach it, and what he would do once he was free from the ship.

Nukahiva was part of Anna Maria Bay and famous among the sailors who put in at the Marquesas. It was shaped like a horseshoe, with a long and narrow entrance between two small, coral islands. The beach was three miles beyond, gently curving, smooth white sand, and almost a mile in length.

A deep and thickly verdured valley rose up from the

beach, stretched back several miles to the mountains. There were waterfalls that dropped with a iridescent smother of spray from side valleys. Breadfruit, pandanus, and palm trees grew along the beach, the bigger trees crested by parasitical growth that attracted bright-colored birds. The valley floor was level, covered with a fine, yellow grass. Among the trees, the palm-thatch roofs of the native huts showed.

The scene matched almost flawlessly the images that Melville had carried in his mind for six years. He had first heard of Nukahiva from his cousin, Thomas Wilson Melville, who served as midshipman aboard U.S.S. *Vincennes*. The Navy ship had spent three weeks in 1829 cruising the Marquesas, and men were given liberty ashore. Thomas Melville was among a group that passed a day in the superbly beautiful Valley of Typee in the interior of the island.

While Herman Melville had lived at his grandfather's home, Broadhall, in Pittsfield, Massachusetts, he talked for hours on end with the former midshipman. Thomas Melville had left the Navy for physical reasons, and he missed the sea, the ships, what he considered the best years of his life. He gave his younger cousin a sense of adventure, a longing for the unknown that was never to be absent from the roots of Herman's thought.

Nukahiva, seen from the oil-slopped, dirty main deck of *Acushnet*, was for him the entrance to a life that should be very much like paradise. He did not by any sign let Captain Pease suspect that he was going to desert. He had known since the beginning of the voyage that in all probability the brig would touch here, and his plan was made. Boat crews hauled water casks and provisions between the beach and the ship. When his turn came to take an oar, he would go up the beach, slip out of sight of the mate, cross the valley to the mountain slopes beyond, and not come back.

But Melville was cautious enough to take a shipmate with him. He proposed to enter the Valley of Typee and live there. It was known to him, although he had not yet passed the information on to his companion, that the inhabitants of Typee were supposed to be cannibals.

The man Melville had picked as his companion was a smart young sailor named Richard Tobias Greene. He was, like Melville, an ordinary seaman. But he came from Rochester in inland New York State, and was aboard the *Acushnet* because he hoped to find a better living as a whaler than he would ashore. He had none of Melville's romantic imagination or spiritual unease to force him from the ship, although he allowed the other to persuade him to desert.

He went with Melville into the work boat at Melville's quiet demand, and they sat on the same thwart while she was rowed to the beach. Then, when the water casks were lifted out and set on log rollers for the trip to the village spring, they stood shoulder to shoulder.

The vast dislike that Melville felt for Captain Pease made him look around at the ship from the edge of the palm grove. He would not have another chance to express his farewell to Pease, he knew. He stared out at the brig, made ugly and squat by her brick tryworks structure midships, and saw that Captain Pease from underneath the poop awning closely regarded the work party through the long-glass. Melville had been tempted to shake his fist, and put a malediction on Pease. Now he kept on steadily into the grove, out of sight of the ship.

Curious and completely naked native children stood around the spring where the casks were filled. Men and women almost as naked stood beside them, smiling, but not friendly, their eyes narrowed with apprehension. Too many whaler crews had landed here, Melville realized. Women had been raped, and infected with venereal disease. There had been drunkenness and fights and theft, wanton disorder.

But none of that would exist in the Valley of Typee. It was too remote, and from the accounts he had heard, the warriors were so fierce that no stranger dared to arouse their anger. Melville nodded to Toby Greene, and indicated the path from the grove toward the village. The young sailor nodded back, and they gradually began to move away from the spring.

The second mate, sweaty, hot, and impatient, was in command of the work party. He dealt with one of the chief's wives in *beche de mer* talk for the sale of breadfruit and did not look around when Melville and Greene started along the path.

The two laughed at each other when they understood that they would not be pursued. Some of Melville's profoundly romantic nature came to the surface, and he shouted songs, scraps of chanteys and hymns, answered bird calls, and told Greene in great detail about the splendid life they would find in Typee.

They were now almost at the end of this outer valley. The mountains closed steeply around them. They had passed the last of the village huts and the little taro patches where the women bent and scratched with wooden hoes. Ferns grew across the trail, high and thick, and there were immense stands of bamboo, and cactus, and plants which Melville could not identify.

Both he and Greene wore duck pants and wide-brimmed tarpaulin hats, were barefoot, and carried their short duck jumpers over their arms. The air here was chill, and they shivered, put on the jumpers. How far was it, Greene wanted to know, from here to Typee?

Herman Melville said that he was not sure. His cousin

had never put him straight about the distance. But it could not be too far. Greene said that maybe they had better go back, down into the outer valley, and spend the night there. If they kept going, they would lose the trail in the dark.

If they went back, Melville said, they would be grabbed by the second mate or Pease himself. Then they would be given twenty apiece of the best from a tarred rope-end, put in the ship's brig for a month on bread and water. Pease was determined not to lose any more men from his ship. She was already very shorthanded.

Greene agreed. He said that he was willing to keep going. No more *Acushnet* for him. But Melville realized that he must tell Greene about the reputation of the Typee natives. They were supposed to be cannibals, although that was not fully confirmed.

Greene said that Melville had picked a fine time to tell him. Night filled the valley. It was impossible to see the trail. There were strange creakings, cries, calls, and disturbances in the jungle. But no wild animals were here, Melville assured him, and no snakes. The fireflies would help them find their way to the top ridge of the mountain. Up where the forest growth was thinner, they could use moonlight, and the stars.

Melville led the way, Greene too tired, hungry, and dispirited to speak. They fell down often along the way, tripped over lianas, stumbled upon rotten logs in thickets which they fought through with their arms raised before their faces. Melville kept his sense of direction only by the fact that they moved upward. They had lost the trail, and he doubted that he would again find it.

Then, though, they emerged to find themselves upon the top ridge, and below them, washed by a sea of moonlight, was Typee. The big fireflies were suddenly pale, and very small. They seemed to disappear. Moonlight held the world and poured through the valley from rim to rim.

The enormous banks of cumulus cloud that formed above every Pacific island massed here in buttresses and pinnacles and sheer, silver-touched walls that trembled with the impact of far-off wind. Melville looked down into the valley, still beneath the moonlight. He saw in imagination the temple where the weird statues of the gods rested, the faces carved in flat, harsh planes, the eyes perpetually staring with an awful hatred, the lips spatulate, and cruel. These gods demanded many sacrifices, some of flesh and human blood.

The village huts were lower in the valley. The chief slept on his mat, an arm tossed over the shoulder of his favorite wife. His war club, with the shark teeth imbedded along the striking edge, was at his side.

The girl, the maiden of whom Melville had often dreamed, was in the next hut. She was one of the chief's daughters. For Melville, she was still nameless. He could see her eyes, though, dark, wide in a moonlight shaft, and the clear brow, the smooth curves of the arms and the body. The girl lay awakened by the moonlight and thought of love. It would be his great good fortune to bring love to her.

Melville began to run down the mountainside from the crest. He jumped from fallen tree to tree, balancing precariously, clutching out at lianas to save himself. Toby Greene protested. He said that Melville was moon-crazy, and should stop.

Melville laughed at him. He kept on, faster. Then he slipped on a lichened log. The jagged, upright end of a broken branch tore through his pants high on the left thigh and penetrated the muscle with an immediate surge of pain. His call was like a scream, and Greene quickly joined him.

Greene cleaned the wound as best he could, then made a tourniquet from strips ripped out of his jumper. He told Melville to lie still and save strength. It would soon be dawn. Then he would go back to the beach at Nukahiva and find help. He could not carry Melville, and he was not going to take the chance of approaching the Typee cannibals when he was alone.

Melville did not attempt to answer. He lay partly delirious with pain, and was not sure when Greene left. But he was aware that it was an hour or so after dawn. He dozed, or entered stupor, came to consciousness near what he calculated to be noon. Greene was not coming back for him, he realized. There were ants crawling up his leg toward the wound. He could not stay here; he would die.

Melville drew himself erect by pulling at the branch that had gashed his thigh. He formed a crutch with pieces of wood and lianas. It took him a long time, all the rest of that day, and on into the night, before he got down the mountainside and into the soft spread of *kunai* grass across the floor of Typee.

Children heard his groans of pain out in the darkness, and thought he was a ghost. They shouted to their parents. Men found him. He was taken to the chief's hut and asked a number of questions that he could not answer. Then the chief gave Melville into the care of his youngest daughter. Melville was not surprised when she walked into the hut. This was the same girl, the one of his dreams. He nodded in his delirium. Her name was Fayaway.

While the days slowly passed, Melville immersed himself in the life of Typee. He sought to understand every phase of it, already aware, if only part-consciously, that he would later write about it. His injured leg had begun to heal with the treatment given by several of the chief's older wives, and Melville was very grateful to them. But, from the first night, he had stayed with the handsome, soft-spoken Fayaway in her hut, and the chief seemed proud of the fact that his daughter had taken the stranger as her lover.

Melville spent a great deal of the daytime hours seated

on a mat outside the door of Fayaway's hut. He learned the language from her, and the ways of her people, and was content that Toby Greene would not return for him, and that no other white men came here to impair the peace of this valley.

Fayaway sat beside him and wove fans of pandanus leaves or ground taro in a hardwood bowl with a masher made of dark volcanic stone. She wore a robe fashioned from *tapa* that reached just beneath her round, full breasts, and red jasmine buds were in her black and smooth hair; her ear pendants were sperm whale teeth that had been finely filigreed.

She told Melville how the men of the tribe went out after bonito, the best of all fish, during the day, and at night by the light of torches caught flying fish. There were many sharks around the reefs where the men worked in their canoes, so their paddles were also fashioned as weapons. These were made of porcupine wood, narrow-bladed, and set with mother of pearl.

Melville wanted to know about the tribe's religion. His vocabulary was now quite large, and he could question Fayaway, understand nearly all of her replies. *Varua ino*, she said, was the earth spirit, and a vague sort of devil. *Tupapau* was the quite terrible god of the ancestors. But she could not speak much more about them. That was *tapu*—forbidden.

Melville changed the conversation. He asked about the stars which cast such brilliance upon the valley at night that shadows could be seen. The constellation called the Scorpion was really a fish, Fayaway said, and had been flung up into the sky in ancient times by Maui, the most powerful of all gods. The Pleiades were called *matariki;* that meant "Little Eyes."

But then Fayaway went off to prepare supper, and Melville sat alone. He watched the almost hairless village dogs, and the rats that came down off the rafters of the huts to sniff at coconut shells. He remembered that Fayaway had told him that the small boys recited a verse when they were ready to lose a first tooth. The boys tossed the tooth out into the bush, and asked, "Thy tooth, thy tooth, oh rat. Give it to the man. The tooth, the tooth of the man I give to the rat."

Melville stood up and tried his injured leg. He wondered again about the fine, high-walled hut of pandanus logs that rested solitary on a rise of land near the village. That was the temple, he knew, and he had seen the chief and a number of the senior warriors gathering there, and once heard the tremendous, deep-toned drum beaten in what he believed to be a summons to worship.

The dogs made periodic visits to the temple, and it was Melville's thought that they were attracted by what was left from sacrifice. He was almost completely convinced that the Typee tribe practiced cannibalism. Fayaway had told him that the tribe's great enemy were the Happars, the people from a nearby valley. The Typee warriors were often absent, and could have gone to the sea for fish, or to raid the Happars, and bring back prisoners for sacrifice.

But Melville stopped his devious, strange pondering about cannibalism. He slept in the sun, his dark-haired head down, his injured leg stretched out on a rolled mat. When he awoke, Fayaway grasped him by the shoulder and said supper was ready.

They ate seated side by side against the hut wall while the dusk leaped down the sky with immense speed. The little, sharp-whistling tattler birds were still; the terns and the mallard ducks were gone for the night. Most of the dogs and all of the children were quiet. Melville ate raw mackerel, roasted breadfruit, taro, yams, sweet potatoes. The food was seasoned with what Fayaway called *tai akari*, a mixture of sea water and coconut sauce which was piquant and very good.

There was a great deal here, Melville realized, that was very good. His puritanical background could not force him to deny that. But he had not done a lick of work since he had been here, and he lived in an open relationship with Fayaway. Perhaps he was losing his entire sense of balance, and all that had been of importance in his life before he entered Typee.

The night fragrance, the vast sweep of the stars, the Trade Wind, soft, warm, and pulsant across the valley through the trees, and some woman singing of love in a half-drowsy voice arrested his thought. He went into the hut with Fayaway and to bed.

Late in the night, though, with the starlight gone and mist thick across the valley, he lay awake. He was once more acutely aware of his surroundings, and in this absolute quiet, oppressed by the knowledge that he was a stranger here.

He could not stay long in Typee. His roots would pull him from the place. The proud, stiff-backed Dutch in him, and the equally proud and puritanical side that came from his father's Scots-English heritage were certain to send him back to Albany, then to Pittsfield, the narrow, cold, and harsh New England life.

There was no way that he could escape. Pride, his father's failure in business, the humiliation of the family afterward, the tremendous strain put upon his mother by the care of eight children, that and his connections with the sea through his uncle and his cousin had brought him here.

His uncle, tough, white-bearded Captain John de Wolf, had sailed to Archangel in North Russia. Then, from the port, he went by dogsled to St. Petersburg in the depth of the savage Russian winter. Captain de Wolf made the bobsled journey in company with Captain G. H. von Langsdorff, the famous explorer.

Herman Melville remembered that, staring out the door of the hut into the Typee valley mist. He even remembered von Langsdorff's initials. The facts of his life, and what had led him here were all very clear. He came from a highly intelligent and extremely well-informed family where every fact of any importance was discussed at length.

When his father had failed in business and then died, his mother became gray-haired with the burden she carried. She took a house for the eight children and herself in Lansingburgh, a suburb of Albany. The river ran near it, and Herman Melville saw there the barges headed into Troy, and the ketches and the sloops and the gundalows that made Albany a port. He went down the river when he was in his late teens, pushed by poverty and following the example of his uncle and his cousin.

He made his first voyage in a deepwater ship from New York, signed aboard the miserable old *Highlander*. The captain handled him adroitly and cheated him out of his wages. He came back to Albany with very little except some terrible memories of dockside Liverpool and a sea vocabulary. Then he took refuge at Broadhall, his grandfather's big house in Pittsfield.

The house had wide lawns and beds of flowers, and the rooms were high-ceilinged. Some of the rooms were entirely lined by bookcases, and there were French paintings, sculptures, a piano. Staying there, he got over the bad effects of the voyage, but he also decided that he must go to sea again.

His next ship was *Acushnet*. Now, here in Typee, he began to understand that he missed Pittsfield. He wanted to return to the beautiful Berkshire valley with its elms and maples and locusts and oaks, trees greater than any in these islands. It would be good to see snow again, and ride a pung along the river road, skate on the ponds in the moonlight.

Melville tried hard to convince himself that the people here were cannibals. That would give him a reason to leave Typee. He dismissed from his mind the possibility that the sacrificial flesh remnants found around the temple came from village pigs which had been ceremoniously slaughtered by a priest. He should get out before he was killed. The people were holding him for sacrifice. Why else was he kept idle, fed, sheltered, given Fayaway to care for all his needs?

Melville left Typee early in August, 1842, telling Fayaway that he was going to the beach at Nukahiva to fish. He had already seen at anchor in the harbor the ship he planned to board. His leg was fully healed and he took along with him a couple of young men from the village, aware that he could get clear from them when he wished. But they remained close beside him as they walked the beach, and he was forced to turn suddenly and strike one of them before he could run toward the whaler's boat that was headed offshore.

Men who talked to him in twanging Yankee accents or broad Cockney helped him into the boat. They said they were sorry to see he had trouble with the natives, but their ship was shorthanded. Melville said that he was an experienced sailor out of the whaling brig *Acushnet*, and wanted to know the name of this ship.

She was the bark *Lucy Ann*, the boat crew told him. Her master was a man named Vinson, who was a landlubber. Her mate was rough and big, but good-natured, and drunk half the time. He was named John Jermin, knew his work, and really ran the ship.

Melville was welcomed without questions when he went aboard *Lucy Ann*. The captain signed him on at once, but only for Papeete, the next port of call. Then, on his way forward to the crew's quarters, Melville began to understand why. He met on the main deck a man who presented himself simply as Long Ghost and explained that he was the former ship's doctor. The captain had recently demoted him, and Long Ghost had moved into the fo'c'sle.

The ship was Australian-owned, Long Ghost told Melville. He had made sure of that the other day, Melville said, when he had seen *Lucy Ann* come into the bay. He was pleased that she was not of American registry, he admitted. His last ship had been American, and her logbook might read that he was a deserter from her.

Long Ghost said that such things did not matter aboard *Lucy Ann*. The ship was in extremely bad shape, and men jumped her in almost every port. She had been condemned two years ago in Sydney, but then was slightly repaired, and sold, sent to sea. Long Ghost suggested that he and Melville should get out of her just as soon as she anchored in Papeete. Life could be very agreeable on the beach there.

Melville realized that he was in conversation with a real South Sea Island rover, what the Polynesians called *omoo*—a beachcomber. Long Ghost had the nasal speech of the Sydney docks, and bragged happily about the years he had spent without work in various parts of the South Seas. He advocated that a young Yankee sailor like Melville, smart and, from his talk, well-educated, join him in future adventures.

Melville was pleased. A man of Long Ghost's raffish, openly unscrupulous character appealed to the restlessness in his own nature. Long Ghost had quite certainly in the past served time in jail, and broken the law in several ways. But he was witty and oddly learned; he could quote Virgil and Hudibras. Here in this ship which Melville had boarded with tremendous haste, he was the one man for whom he had any liking.

The crew of *Lucy Ann* were South Seas misfits, men who sailed from one port to the next, and changed ships more often than they changed shirts. The ship herself astounded Melville, who with all his hatred of her, remembered *Acushnet* as fundamentally sound.

This two-hundred-ton vessel was in reality a floating coffin. While the crew which Melville had joined took her from Nukahiva to Papeete he discovered that her lower masts were dangerously weak, and both her standing and running rigging were sorely worn. Parts of her bulwarks were rotten, and about to collapse. The fo'c'sle was like nothing Melville had ever seen before, or imagined.

He described it later: "It looked like the hollow of an old tree going to decay. In every direction the wood was damp and discolored, and here and there soft and porous. Moreover, it was hacked and hewed without mercy, the cook frequently helping himself to splinters for kindling wood from butts and beams."

Rations aboard *Lucy Ann* were scanty, and bad. They consisted of condemned Royal Navy stores bought at auction in Sydney. There had been, Melville discovered, thirty-two men in the original crew. Twelve of those were deserters, among them three mates and three harpooners. More than half of the remaining muster were sick and unfit for duty. The captain soon earned Melville's contempt at sea because of his lack of seamanly knowledge. Melville called him Paper Jack—all of the man's right to authority was contained in the ship's papers.

Melville, Long Ghost, and some of the other seamen tried to get out of the ship in Papeete. They appealed to the British consul and swore that she was dangerously unseaworthy. The captain answered the charge by an accusation of mutiny, and they were put in the Broom Road jail, renowned throughout the South Seas as Calabooza Beratanee. That distinction, Melville realized, was given because most of the inmates were subjects of Great Britain, and a Calabooza was just *beche de mer* translation from the Spanish word for jail.

Life in the Calabooza was pleasant enough. The men had been allowed to take their sea-chests ashore with them, and they bartered the contents for food, tobacco, and a little rum. Then, after a few weeks of confinement, the big, fat and good-natured jailer came into the room the prisoners occupied in common. He gave them the news in emphatic *beche de mer*, "Ah, my boy! Shippy you haree—maky sail!"

So *Lucy Ann* had picked up a crew of sorts and gone back to sea to hunt whale. That meant no charges would be pressed against them here, and they were free. Melville and Long Ghost walked out into Broom Street and headed for the waterfront, source of practically all evil for them, but also the place where other drifters like themselves could get information, a free meal, and if they were not too lazy, work.

Melville and his companion retained enough initiative after the month in jail to take jobs on the nearby island of Eimeo. They crossed to it in a native canoe, and changed their names temporarily to Peter and Paul. They did not want to be known as mutineers when they landed. The jobs offered them were at the big State of Maine mission farm, and Long Ghost suggested that it would serve no purpose to prejudice the manager's appraisal of them.

But the work was digging potatoes for twelve hours a day under the cruel Polynesian sun. Lanky and fair-haired Long Ghost refused to continue with it, although the more powerfully built Melville had not found it too onerous. Long Ghost used his best diction as he informed the manager that digging potatoes was not what he should really do to forward the affairs of the mission. He suggested that he be given a rifle; it would be easy for him, an expert shot, to kill a considerable number of the wild cattle on the land that adjoined the mission. Long Ghost was quick to say that the cattle belonged to Queen Pomare, but she was wealthy and would never miss them.

Long Ghost served briefly as a sharpshooter while Melville stayed in the fields at hard labor. The work was a kind of anodyne for Melville. It dulled the pain of his separation from Fayaway and the life in the Valley of Typee. He was now completely adrift, and aware of it. Still, he could sense that he would inevitably return to New England; loneliness would take him there, and the vast inner need to end his wandering in a circumstance where he might find peace.

The mission manager dismissed him and Long Ghost without comment but with very little pay. They did not argue and wandered on across the beautiful island from the mission at Matai to Taloo, where Queen Pomare was supposed to visit. Sleeping while the sun was high, walking the flowered lanes in the cool hours and bartering for food or begging it from the genial Polynesians, they came to Taloo and went on further to another village named Papetoai.

Long Ghost had the idea that they could install themselves quite readily in the favor of Queen Pomare. Just let him, he told Melville, present her with one of his more eloquent speeches and she would make him her prime minister. Melville could take over the job of minister of marine.

Melville was very far from the background in which he had attended Albany Academy, been a member of the Juvenile Total Abstinence Association and the Anti-Smoking Society. He went boldly with Long Ghost to the house which Queen Pomare occupied and broke in upon her. They offered no warning, and found the large, matronly woman seated at dinner.

The queen wore a loose cotton gown, Melville noticed,

and she was bareheaded and barefooted. Her dinner, spread
out before her on the floor, was breadfruit, poi, coconuts, and
roast pig. It was very savory and rested on leaves that served
as dishes.

But Queen Pomare sharply resented their presence. She
called to some of her women before Long Ghost could begin
his speech of proposal for office. The women appeared, and
waved the pair of beachcombers from the house. Melville
finally felt a flick of shame. His mother and his sisters would
not be pleased if they knew what had happened here.

Melville parted from Long Ghost soon after that. There
was an American whaler, the brig *Julia*, in the harbor at
Taloo. Melville went aboard and talked with her master, who
came from Martha's Vineyard. He was willing to ship Melville, the captain said, but not Long Ghost. His term for Long
Ghost was "a Sydney bird," and Melville knew that jailbird
was meant. The type was common in the island ports, and unmistakable, Melville realized. If he wanted to get home, here
was his chance, and he signed articles aboard *Julia*. Then,
without much real regret, he went ashore to say good-bye to
Long Ghost.

Melville sailed in *Julia* as an ordinary seaman for several
months while she worked back and forth across the Line in
pursuit of whale. Then she put into Honolulu in March, 1843,
and he signed off her articles, took his pay, and went on the
beach. He was fully headed home now; the need to return
was too acute to be denied.

He was on the beach in Honolulu for four months before
he could ship out homeward-bound aboard the United States
Navy frigate *United States*. She was a cruelly hard-disciplined
ship after the almost carelessly handled whalers in which he
had sailed. But he was a highly competent seaman, instantly
obeyed the petty officers in his watch, kept out of the way of

the commissioned officers. The Navy for him was just a means of getting home.

He was discharged at Boston in October, 1844, and went back to Pittsfield. He had been away from home almost four years. His life had gone full orbit, and he was glad that he had left the sea.

Melville began to write almost as soon as he was settled ashore. He told of the Valley of Typee, and of Fayaway, and the sacrifices that he had never seen but could most vividly imagine. His first book, *Typee*, was an instant success. He wrote a second which was called *Omoo*, and told of his wanderings with Long Ghost.

He kept on with other books, and the former castaway and beachcomber was now a major figure in the literary circles of New York. He married in 1847 a New England girl who was the daughter of a Supreme Court justice. He made a trip to England in 1849 to arrange for publication of his work, and visited Paris. Then, the next year, he and his wife went to the northwest part of Massachusetts to live. They occupied a farmhouse which was to be their home for thirteen years and where he wrote *Moby-Dick*.

Nathaniel Hawthorne was staying nearby when Melville started work in 1851 on *Moby-Dick*. The two men were soon close friends, and Hawthorne, brought up in Salem and the son of a sea captain, recognized the tremendous power that Melville possessed. He encouraged the moody, introspective ex-whaler, and as a consequence Melville dedicated the book to him. It was the greatest expression of gratitude that Melville could offer his friend. *Moby-Dick* contained without doubt his very best writing. The years that he had spent at sea had now become invaluable.

The unhesitating, implacable morality involved made the decision fantastically cruel. Captain Edward Edwards, Royal Navy, was himself a castaway, and had just survived a long and perilous voyage in a small boat across the wastes of the Southwest Pacific. Still, he was ready to take the young woman, her sick husband, and two little children, one an infant, back to England as his prisoners.

They and their companions were escaped convicts from the Australian penal settlement at Port Jackson, near Botany Bay. There was no doubt about identity, or the illegality of their presence here on Timor. Edwards was absolutely certain of his duty *to His Majesty and to English law. The possibility of mercy did not complicate his thought. The other prisoners he conducted to England despite shipwreck, great hazards at sea afterward, and lack of sufficient crew to guard them, were the last of the mutineers from HMS* Bounty *left on Tahiti.*

Captain Edwards was a very determined man. He went at once to the Dutch governor and requested that the English people who had landed recently on Timor be put in his custody. They must be returned to England, all of them, so that justice would be correctly exercised.

MARY BRYANT

MARY BRYANT sat in the boat for some minutes after it was free of the surf and had been hauled up onto the beach. The smaller child, Emmanuel, was in her arms, and Charlotte rested on the thwart beside her. She was not sure of the reason; she was so fatigued that her thought was incoherent, but she believed that she stayed in the boat with the children because it was familiar, familiar and safe. The boat had just brought them across 1,200 miles of open ocean.

Mary Bryant looked up and smiled at her husband. She was no longer afraid, she told herself. She was ready to go ashore. She spoke gently to Charlotte. The little girl, scrawny in her faded cotton dress, her legs raw with sea boils, her hair lank with the spindrift from the surf, climbed staggering from the boat.

Charlotte turned on the dark volcanic sand, her hands stretched to help her mother. Mary Bryant felt a pang of longing that broke through the barrier against emotion that she had erected in her mind. Her daughter was four, the baby less than a year. They did not deserve this. Life should be better for them.

Mary Bryant stepped ashore and realized at once that her feet were splayed, bore the scars of coral scratches and sea boils. She made a strange, almost laughable figure. Her shoes had been discarded months ago. The dress she wore was ragged, very short, and in England, even in Botany Bay, would be called immodest. She might shock some of the Dutchmen here.

But modesty was for her a word like home, and rest, and peace. They were as far away as the stars her husband used to navigate the boat. She swung Emmanuel up onto her hip, pushed back her salt-sticky hair and walked quickly across the beach.

Her husband stood a few yards off from the other men of the party. He faced the trail that led inland. It had been his intention right from the beginning of the voyage to land here on Timor. But none of them knew what to expect on this island.

Will Bryant had chosen to make his landfall here because the Dutch owned it, and not the British. There was a garrison, with a governor and some Dutch East Indies Company officials, at a place called Coupang. That was farther on, maybe forty miles more along the coast. The Dutchmen might trust them, or at least have mercy.

They were escaped convicts from Botany Bay. If the Dutch governor discovered the fact, he could send them back to Australia where they would serve out their sentences for life. But Will Bryant had a story ready about them being the survivors of a ship lost at sea. They had all of them gone over it during the terrible weeks of the voyage, and even the girl, Charlotte, understood what she was supposed to say when she was questioned.

Mary Bryant sat down on the beach, weak with hunger, the baby in her arms, Charlotte beside her. She watched her husband anxiously, waiting for him to give some sign that meant the trail was safe. But he remained motionless, and she remembered that the entire group was weak with hunger, and that none of them carried a weapon. That trail might lead to some sort of ambush set by the local natives.

They had escaped from many along the fierce coasts of northeastern Australia when storm drove their small, open boat inshore or they were forced to enter the wilderness in search of water. This was early in June, 1791, and it was sixty-nine days since they had left Botany Bay. They had rowed, sailed, hauled, or pushed the six-oared boat for 3,254 miles.

Mary Bryant looked aside at the men who had made the voyage under her husband's command. They were a scarecrow lot, their eyes redshot from the sea glare, their beards and hair long, holes in the elbows and at the knees and thighs of their stained, ripped clothing. There was James Cox, who had helped her husband plan the voyage; and William Allen; and John Butcher; James Martin; Nathaniel Lilly; William Morton, who was exceptionally strong and tough, a man with rawhide muscles; and John Simms. Each of them had proven himself brave and done his share of work at sea and inshore.

Will Bryant, who was Cornwall-born and a fisherman by trade, took the responsibility for the navigation. He was the man who slipped aboard the Dutch ship in Port Jackson, near Botany Bay, and bought the quadrant, the compass, and the chart. So the others agreed that he should be their leader and allowed him to bring along his wife and the two children.

The officers and men of the New South Wales Corps that guarded the penal settlement were corrupt, took a steady toll of bribes from the convicts. It was not hard to buy a pair of muskets, powder and shot, eight gallons of water, a hundred pounds of flour and a hundred pounds of rice, fourteen pounds of salt pork, tallow, soap, rope, a grapnel anchor, and a few more essential stores. The escape from Botany Bay, made at night and with the connivance of the harbor guards, was not hard. The danger came later, when Will Bryant took the boat offshore and started to the northward on the course that was to end at Timor.

Storm beat at the boat. She badly leaked, and time after time very nearly sank. The people aboard sat submerged waist-deep. Mary Bryant crouched silent, her infant son in her arms, Charlotte at her side. Bailing took some of the water out of the boat, and Will Bryant was able to steer. But he was forced to head inshore, and at night, on a lightless coast that was almost unexplored.

He put the grapnel anchor down to hold the boat away from the breakers that would certainly sink her. The strain on the anchor line was so great, though, that it parted, and the boat was caught by the inshore surge. The men rowed, and kept the boat alive through the surf, made a landing on the beach.

But, soon after dawn, while the men paid the leaky seams of the boat with tallow, the natives came out of the brush above the beach. The natives had waited for full light to use their bows and their flat-bladed spears. Will Bryant picked up a musket, quickly fired it. The natives stood still while the ball whirled humming overhead.

The party had time to reverse and load the boat, then get aboard. But frizzy-headed warriors followed out from the beach, screaming with fury and throwing spears until they were shoulders-deep in the surf. That sort of attack continued throughout the rest of the voyage until Will Bryant brought the boat into the Straits of Endeavour at the northernmost part of Australia.

The formidable stretch of the Great Barrier Reef, almost 1,000 miles of coral heads, cross-currents, and whirlpool eddies, was astern. The last charge of the screaming Bushmen had been avoided. But here in the breadth of the Gulf of Carpentaria, when Will Bryant sent the boat toward shore, huge outrigger war canoes appeared. The escaped people sought fresh water and any kind of crayfish or limpets. They were literally dying of hunger. Will Bryant was forced to sheer off from the shore.

The war canoes held as many as thirteen men armed with bows, spears, and clubs. Bryant hoisted both mainsail and jib aboard the boat. He tacked carefully, taking every advantage of the wind, until the canoes were to leeward, and the boat was safe from attack. It was hours later, though, before he could close with the shore and men could go on the beach to find water.

Then, the water cask full, a little food aboard, Bryant shaped the course for Timor. It was the final gamble. When the boat reached Timor, he could not do any more. They could not sail farther than that. The boat was in too poor shape. The rest, if they were to go free, depended on luck.

Mary Bryant saw the warning gesture her husband made and stood up, ready to run back to the boat. Men advanced from the trail onto the beach. They were natives, and Will Bryant spoke to them in scraps of Dutch and English, made sign talk.

The natives were tall and dark-skinned, with regular features, long, prominent noses, and bushy growths of hair that spread out widely from their heads. They wore loose cotton garments, the lower piece wrapped around the body like a skirt, and only one of them was armed, carried a fish spear.

Will Bryant told the prepared story. The people with him, he explained, were survivors from an English ship lost at sea. He was the ship's supercargo. During the storm that had sunk the vessel, their boat was separated from the others, and they had found their own way to Timor.

The natives gravely inclined their heads in understanding. They indicated that the people of the party leave the beach and go along the trail with them. Mary Bryant walked swaying, the sea heave still in her legs. Then, in the little village where the native men led them, she recognized how much she had suffered during the voyage.

Some of the women there broke down and wept at sight of her. She was offered food, clothing, palm wine, and made to sit in a hut where she could wash, clean her hair. The boils on Charlotte's legs were lanced and bandaged. The child got a new dress and a turban against the sun, and a piece of sugar coconut to suck. Emmanuel was bathed and fed, and fell quickly asleep next to his mother.

These were the first women with whom Mary Bryant had been since leaving Botany Bay. She was profoundly grateful for their company, was almost overcome by their kindness. But her husband came into the hut and told her they must go on to Coupang. The headman of this village was responsible to the Dutch governor, and would take them there.

Mary Bryant got up at once and said that she was ready to leave. She and the children felt much better. They would make the march all right.

The party walked through the late hours of the day along trails that flanked irrigation ditches, maize fields, and rice paddies. The village headman rode a small horse and held a cutlass which he brandished to show the strangers the sights. But Mary Bryant noticed that the men gave him short, vague answers. They sensed Will Bryant's tension, she realized, and were worried by it.

Mary Bryant came from Fowey, in Cornwall. She shared the same background as her husband, was responsive to his moods. It was obvious to her now that Will Bryant was under severe nervous strain. Muscles flexed in his throat and jaws. A vein pulsed blue and prominent in the right side of his temple. He had pushed himself to the extreme limits of his strength to bring them safe to Timor, she knew, and if they met further hard luck at Coupang, her man might not be able to take it.

Mary Bryant was twenty-six years old, but she had not been in church since her late teens, had forgotten how to pray. There was nothing to do, she told herself, except hope for the best at Coupang. Then, to relieve her own tension, she watched her daughter.

Charlotte was the only one in the group who admired the island beauty. It amazed her after the desolate expanses of the sea. Thrushes flew from the underbrush, and kingfishers and orioles were overhead; parrots pecked at mangoes. Great trees were along the road, and Charlotte wanted to know their names. Then it was dark, though, and the baby weighed heavily on Mary Bryant's hip, and she walked with dragging strides. The headman took them to a village which he said was close to Coupang, and arranged for the group to sleep in a large hut. The castaways were too tired to eat or think about eating, almost immediately fell asleep, Will Bryant at Mary's side.

Bryant swapped a knife for food in the morning, got bowls of rice, grated coconut, and some mangosteens for it.

The headman who served as guide supervised the deal, and after the party was fed proudly pointed across the trees. That was Coupang.

The church spire showed above the treetops. When the party was on the road again and had walked for a mile or so, they could see the whitewashed walls of the Dutch bungalows. There was a flagstaff at the fort, and a drum was being ruffled, commands were shouted.

Native soldiers came first from the fort, barefoot and in loose formation. They stood around the castaways and stared. Then a young Dutch officer in jackboots gray with dust arrived. He was followed by another, older officer who rode a horse and spoke English.

Will Bryant spoke quietly with the senior officer. He said that they were castaways from an English ship, a brig that had foundered two hundred miles offshore in the Timor Sea. He was the ship's supercargo. These men were sailors. The woman and the children had been passengers aboard.

The Dutch officer saluted when Will Bryant finished the story. He gestured and started his horse forward into the town. The party began to move, Bryant beside his wife. He said that the officer had gone to tell *Mynheer* Timotheus Wanjon, the governor, that they were here. Their story, up until this moment, was believed.

Mynheer Wanjon was florid-faced and stuffed in a tight uniform. But he was polite, even friendly, agreed at once to let Will Bryant buy food and clothing for the members of the party and charge the cost to the British government. The governor's wife welcomed Mary Bryant with great sympathy, sent her in charge of a Malay woman servant to a bedroom in a wing of the big bungalow.

Charlotte and the baby were put in a trundle bed and soon went to sleep in the cool, shadowed room. Mary Bryant washed herself, then put on the clean cotton dress brought her by the servant. She stretched out on the huge four-poster Dutch bed beside the trundle bed, shut her eyes, and tried to sleep.

But this was the first time she had been really clean in months. She had never been in a bed that was so comfortable since she had left home in Fowey. Memory was opened for her, and she recalled the details of what had brought her to Botany Bay as a convict, then to the attempt at escape which had proved almost more than her strength could take.

Back in Fowey, on a summer night, she and three other village girls had got hold of some fermented cider and drank it just to be merry, have a bit of fun. The others were Catherine Fryer, Mary Haydon, and Mary Shepherd. All of them came from poor families, worked hard in the fields and at home. They were shouting, singing, and dancing along the King's Highway after dark when they met Miss Lakeman.

Miss Lakeman was the village spinster. They were young, and a little tipsy. She sniffed and tried to hurry past and said that she would report them to their parents. Their temptation was to laugh at her. But they already had a reputation as hoydens, and the threat made them angry. So they slapped her, snatched her bonnet from her head, took her reticule and her mittens, chased her down the highway while she clutched her skirts and screeched like a seagull.

The arrests were made the next morning. The technical charge, the constable explained to Mary's father, was highway robbery with violence. It was punishable by hanging. Mary's father, William Broad, was a sailor and a husky man. He started for the constable, and his wife tried to restrain him. The constable was forced to call for help before he could take Mary off to Fowey jail.

When she was tried at the next Assizes, the judges did not hesitate in sentencing her. She was told that she received clemency; she was not to be hanged. Her sentence was transportation for life to the penal colony at New Holland.*

It was during the voyage out to Botany Bay in the prison ship that she met Will Bryant. He was a former fisherman who had run afoul of the law when at his trade on the Cornish coast. His sentence was only for seven years, but very few convicts were ever able to return to England. The British government wished the colony to grow and become permanent. Mary and Will Bryant fell in love aboard the prison ship, and were married by the chaplain. Both of the children were born under the primitive conditions of convict life in the colony. They, too, would be prisoners until their parents somehow got fully free from British law.

The castaways had been at Coupang for two weeks when the pair of Royal Navy boats arrived. The craft worked their way through the surf. The crews waded ashore, hauling the boats, and identified themselves to the Dutch soldiers who met them on the beach.

Mary Bryant was seated with her husband and the other castaways in the shade of a mango tree near the village church. They were relaxed, unaware of any danger. Mary had left her children with the Malay woman servant at *Mynheer* Wanjon's house. She was more watchful than the men, saw the big Dutch ship captain as he trotted toward them.

The Dutchman was self-important because he could speak English and served the governor as interpreter. Now he moved much too fast for the heat. He panted with excitement when he reached the group.

Boats from an English ship sunk at sea had just reached

---

* *The name at that time for Australia.*

the beach, he said. A hundred men, maybe more, were in them. "Your captain is here," he said.

Will Bryant started to speak, but he was too late. Nathaniel Lilly jumped up and said, "What captain? Damn me, we have no captain!"

The Dutchman did not wait long after that. He went back at a trot to the governor's house. Will Bryant hit Lilly a blow alongside the head. He called him a stupid swine, and said that Lilly had betrayed them. The Dutchman would tell *Mynheer* Wanjon exactly what had been said here.

Mary Bryant got between her husband and Lilly. She was afraid that her husband would kill the man. But then Bryant laughed. He opened his hands and pointed toward the governor's house.

The uniform was unmistakable. All of them in this group knew every detail, every button and bit of gold lace on it. Their hatred had established it forever in memory. It was worn by a captain of the British Royal Navy. The captain stood beside *Mynheer* Wanjon, the interpreter close, and gazed squinting in the sunlight at them.

Nathaniel Lilly broke and ran. He said that the Royal Navy would never take him back to Botany Bay. He'd die first, by his own hand.

The castaways stood unmoving. They were held by shock. Lilly's stupid talk, and now his running away, finished any chance of escape. They would be taken back to Botany Bay. There was nothing they could do.

Other Royal Navy officers had joined the captain. They were armed with swords and pistols. One of them at a command from the captain walked along the street followed by a pair of Royal Marines with muskets.

Will Bryant cursed. He pushed his wife, and told her to run while there was still time. Dutch troops were joining the

Royal Marines. *Mynheer* knew very well that this lot was escaped convicts, and not survivors from a sunken ship.

Mary Bryant ran, ducking through the neat rows of gravestones in the churchyard and then from tree to tree until she was past the last house in the village. She stopped beneath the broad spread of a banyan tree. She was stunned by grief, said nothing to Lilly when he moved through the woods to her side. They stood there wordless until some Malay soldiers led by a Dutch sergeant found them.

The sergeant took them to the village. They were met near the graveyard by a tall and thin-faced Royal Navy lieutenant. His uniform was stained with sea mold, and his boot soles were loose from the uppers. Still, he was absolutely self-assured.

He said that he was Lieutenant Hayward, lately of His Majesty's frigate *Pandora*. He had orders from Captain Edward Edwards of the Royal Navy to arrest them on suspicion of being escaped convicts from the Botany Bay settlement.

Lilly kept silent. But Mary Bryant gave her name. There was no harm in that, she thought. She stared at Lieutenant Hayward and asked him what brought Royal Navy people to Timor, and by what right was she being held in arrest?

Anger had driven away her fear. She was thinking of her children and what would happen to them under these new conditions. They might be taken from her if she was put in prison before being sent back to Botany Bay.

The lieutenant sensed her anger, and a strange kind of respect came into his voice. He answered her with much more courtesy than he had shown before. *Pandora* had been sent from England to round up the mutineers from His Majesty's Ship *Bounty*, he said. Ten of them had been found on Tahiti and were prisoners; they were being taken back to England for trial. *Pandora* was lost in the Torres Strait. The rest of the voyage here to Timor was made in the ship's boats.

Mary Bryant started to speak and stopped herself. She could get nothing more from this man. There were hundreds of islands where the people from *Pandora* might have landed. But the captain had picked Timor, and without knowing what he was about at first, caught them, the poor, hard-luck lot of convicts. If he was taking the *Bounty* mutineers to England for trial, then they would go, too. They would be tried again in England and given new sentences to be worked out in Australia.

Mary Bryant walked slowly toward the governor's bungalow. The lieutenant was behind her with Lilly, and he half-dragged the man. She was ashamed of Lilly. All of the strength had gone out of him, and during the voyage he had been one of the best in the boat. Still, this was a miserable setback for all of them, and she did not know yet how Will Bryant had taken it.

The Royal Navy captain stood alone on the front porch of the bungalow. His hand was on his sword hilt. He stood with his head back and his feet spread. Mary Bryant gave him a glare of hatred. Maybe she was wrong to do so, she thought. But men like him were the kind that treated her people without mercy. It wouldn't matter much if he held a personal dislike for her. There'd be little change in him, and none in the system.

He spoke to her sharply, said that he was Captain Edward Edwards of His Majesty's Navy. So he had the right to question her, a British subject. He wanted to learn, without lies or elaboration, why she was here, and why she had left the limits of the penal settlement at Botany Bay.

Mary Bryant shook her head. She had nothing to tell him, she said. Captain Edwards gazed at her narrow-eyed. She was to go and get her children, he said, and take them to the cell-block in the fort. Whatever she might have to tell him was of little importance. There had already been a number of confessions from the escaped convicts, among them one from her husband, Will Bryant. Enough was known about her to make her return certain. She would spend the rest of her life at Botany Bay.

Captain Edwards wanted to hurt her, Mary Bryant realized. That was his way. He hated her because she refused to show fear.

She felt it, though. It dazed her, and she went numbly into the shadowed rooms of the bungalow. She wondered again what would happen to her children, and to Will Bryant. If they were separated from her, that would be the end of everything.

She made herself act with calm as she entered the room where the children were. Emmanuel slept, but Charlotte was awake. She took the baby in her arms and asked Charlotte to walk beside her and not to talk.

Outside, in the sunlight on the crushed coral of the walk, a detail of Dutch soldiers waited. They closed around her and the children. Captain Edwards watched from the porch. He stood in the same position, his hand on his sword hilt. He was like a statue, Mary Bryant thought, and part of him was stone. That was his heart.

The entire English company sailed for Batavia on October 6, 1791, in charge of Captain Edwards. He had arranged passage aboard the Dutch ship *Rembang,* and the convict group took its place in the lower hold with the mutineers. All of them were fettered and chained except Mary Bryant and the children. She moved as close as she could to the beam of sunlight that came down from the hatchway above, and talked the guards into giving her an old piece of canvas to cover the children at night.

But she was greatly worried by her husband. He lay in a sort of apathetic stupor, would barely speak to her or Charlotte. The baby still interested him, and he smiled a bit when she brought Emmanuel to him. During the hour from four to five in the afternoon when the prisoners were allowed on deck, he was so weak, though, that the guards had to help him up the ladders. The surgeon from *Pandora*, a man named Hamilton, examined him and said he suffered from a mild fever.

Mary Bryant knew that it was worse than any fever. Her husband had given up completely; he wanted to die. The will to live had left him after they had been captured at Coupang. All of his strength, all of his hope had gone into the escape.

Then, as the Dutch ship was abreast of Bali, there was a night of terrific storm. The sailors closed the hatch tight against the waves. The frames and planks of the hull trembled. Rats chattered in fear and ran back and forth among the people, snapping and biting. One of the *Bounty* mutineers yelled into the darkness that they should be released—they would drown here.

Mary Bryant sat with her baby in her arms. He lay still, exhausted by fright. There was little chance for him, she knew, unless she could get better food. The only ration was sour beer, salt meat, and rice.

The ship put into Samarang after the storm, and Hamilton, the surgeon, entered the hold. Mary Bryant asked to have her husband and the baby sent ashore. They should both be given hospital treatment. Hamilton agreed. But he couldn't grant the permission, he told her. It must come from Captain Edwards, who had already refused Hamilton's own request.

The ship continued to Batavia and anchored. Hospital orderlies requested by Hamilton went into the hold and carried out Bryant and the baby. But Hamilton stayed on deck. He could not bring himself to face Mary Bryant. Permission for her to go ashore to the hospital had been denied by Edwards.

Mary Bryant stayed in the hold for hours. Then, finally, Hamilton came down the ladders. Permission for her and her daughter to go ashore had just been granted, he said. The wives of some Dutch officials had made inquiries ashore and protested to Captain Edwards. They said it was an outrage for her to be kept aboard while members of her family lay ill in the hospital.

Mary Bryant thanked the surgeon. She took Charlotte by the hand and climbed up onto deck. A boat was waiting alongside and they got into it, were rowed to the landing stage.

There was a Dutch doctor at the hospital who spoke English. The pastor of the church was with him. Mary Bryant went aside with the doctor and he told her that her son had died, and that her husband was very ill. She nodded, and said that he was maybe better off dead, the little one. But she would like to see her husband.

Will Bryant was conscious. She sat next to him for a while and held his hand. But he lay still, without talking, and she told him that she would come back and visit him tomorrow.

When she went out into the lobby, the Dutch doctor asked her to sign her son's death certificate. She couldn't write, she said, but she would make her mark. She asked them the date, and the clerk who was with the doctor said it was December 1, 1791. Mary Bryant thanked them and walked back to the landing, Charlotte at her side, and took the boat to the ship.

Her husband died three weeks later in the Batavia hospital. The Dutch pastor insisted upon a funeral, and she agreed. She took part in the simple ceremony at the grave, and some women from the town had arranged for flowers.

Mary Bryant was not allowed ashore after that. Captain Edwards had settled the transportation problem for people in his charge. They were to be sent to Table Bay in four groups aboard Dutch East Indies Company ships. Edwards would take personal command of them again at the Cape of Good Hope, get them shipped on from there to England.

Mary Bryant was sent with Charlotte into a ship called *Hoornwey*. Some of the men who had made the escape from Botany Bay were assigned to the same vessel. It was good to be with her, they said. They were glad to remember how she had acted during the voyage to Timor.

That made her feel better. She lost some of her deep despair. For hours at a time, she sat and talked with James Cox.

Cox was a lifer, sentenced May 24, 1784, at the Exeter Assizes. He had met a young and pretty convict named Sarah Young in Botany Bay. He fell in love with her and wanted to marry her. But Sarah was a loose woman. She gave her favors to several men, and when Cox discovered it he asked to join the escape party that Will Bryant had started to organize.

Bryant accepted him at once, and Cox was helpful in getting supplies for the boat. The last night before the escape, with all their plans made, Cox, who was illiterate, asked Bryant to write a note for him. It was to be left for Sarah Young, and he dictated it: "Do you give over those vices that I have caught you at more than once, or you will come to a bad end."

Here in the hold of the big Dutch East Indiaman, the words returned to Cox. He quoted them to Mary Bryant. That was all far away, he said, and didn't count any more.

But when he went on deck, he flung himself over the side and drowned.

William Morton was the next of the convicts to go. She sat beside him and tried to recall memories that would restore his courage. There were the giant sea turtles they had found on the beaches when they were starving, and the sea coal that lay in loose chunks and made huge, roaring fires when they were dismally wet and cold. Then the fights with the natives which they had miraculously won, and the fish that they caught when starving, and the booby birds that came obligingly enough to perch on the bow of the boat.

Morton listened, and smiled at her, turned his head aside, and died.

When the ship's main yard had been backed and the shrouded and shotted body committed to the deep, Mary Bryant decided to spend her time on deck. She must give more time to Charlotte. If luck went against her in England at her new trial, the people of the court would find some kind of a ward for Charlotte.

Mary Bryant sat all day long in the sunshine with Charlotte at her side. Lieutenant Hayward was in charge of this group of prisoners, but he ignored them. Mary sewed clothes for herself and the child, washed whenever she could get a bucket of water. Her health improved, and Charlotte became tan and almost plump. The Dutch ship was clean, well-handled, the crew sympathetic. Mary and her daughter received many little gifts of fruit, sugar, and bread from the sailors.

HMS *Gorgon* was at anchor in Table Bay when the Dutch ship that carried the prisoners came in under the lee of the huge brown cape. There was a lot of boat traffic between the ships and then, under marine guard, the men still fettered, they were transferred to the Royal Navy frigate. They were

to go to England in *Gorgon*, Lieutenant Hayward said, although the ship was already loaded to the bulwarks with
home-leave troops.

Mary Bryant recognized the rough accents of the women
as she climbed the frigate's ladder with Charlotte. These were
the wives of the New South Wales Corps. The regiment had
been in garrison at Botany Bay during her time there, and
among the convicts was known as the Rum Puncheon Corps.
Officers, noncoms, and privates, their wives and their mis-
tresses were busy in smuggling, making, and selling rum. All
three operations were illegal under British law, but that did
not mean much in Botany Bay. Now, those who had kept
from drinking up the profits went back happy and prosperous
to England.

There were 109 officers and men of the New South
Wales Corps aboard *Gorgon*, with twenty-five wives and
forty-seven children. Pet kangaroos and koalas owned by
various officers were also aboard, and the quarterdeck was
banked with tropical flowers, shrubs, and plants. There was
space made in the corners of the lower hold for the prisoners
who at Captain Edwards' order were fettered and chained.
But Mary Bryant stayed on deck, found a bit of space for
Charlotte and herself near the main hatch.

Gorgon sailed on April 6, 1792 for England. Her master,
Captain John Parker, had his wife aboard with him, and she
entertained the senior ladies of the New South Wales Corps.
The great subject of conversation for the duration of the
passage was Mary Bryant.

It was frowned upon by the major's wife as unfit for
conversation, but all of the other officers' wives engaged in it.
The story of her escape in the boat from Botany Bay was
severely distorted. The mutiny aboard *Bounty*, the capture of
some of the *Bounty* men, the wreck of *Pandora*, and the cap-

ture of the convicts on Timor by Captain Edwards were
mixed into a weird fricassee of melodrama.

Some of the officers' wives insisted that Mary Bryant had
fed her baby at the breast while in the open boat and closely
surrounded by gloating convicts. Then, in another version,
she led the escape. She was the captain. Her husband was a
weakling; she kept a pistol at his back most of the time while
he worked out the navigation. When the party was cast away
on Timor, she twitched around in a wanton fashion in her
torn dress and was able to make a fool of the Dutch governor.
Captain Edwards had ended that ploy. The Royal Navy was
a good bit smarter about such things.

Down in the cramped quarters shared by the soldiers and
their wives, there were other and more erotic versions. Mary
Bryant wasn't Mary Bryant at all. She was a youth, and for his
own reasons—which could be easily guessed—he wore woman's clothing. Aye, one of them. But, if not, and she was a
woman right enough, then to go off in an open boat with
eight men was just too much. Mary Bryant was a common
hussy, an unpaid prostitute.

Mary Bryant was dimly aware of the curiosity she
created. She recognized the meaning of the long, narrow
glances given her from the quarterdeck when the officers'
wives gathered. Some of the bawdy, nasty talk reached her
directly from the soldiers' quarters when discussions were
heated by rum. But Charlotte was ill, and that fact dominated
nearly all of Mary Bryant's thought.

When the ship moved up into the colder latitudes the
child's health rapidly failed. She did not play on deck any
more, or exclaim at the silver flicker of the flying fish, or ask
to have the sailors' work explained. The surgeon examined
her at Mary Bryant's request, and said he did not know of

any cure. But he would leave some medicine, and he believed that Charlotte would be all right.

Then, after a feverish, restless night, at six o'clock in the morning of May 6, the child died. Mary Bryant sat holding Charlotte. She called to a sailor who passed along the deck and he reported to the officer of the watch.

The perfunctory funeral service was given with the main yard backed and the big, broad-hulled frigate stopped in the water. Mary Bryant sat alone, her grief terrible beyond the limits of pain. She did not hear Captain Tench when he came down from the quarterdeck and stood beside her. The tall, broad-shouldered Royal Marine was forced to say his name several times before she recognized that he was there. "Watkin Tench," he said. "In charge of the guard aboard the *Gorgon*."

She looked up and nodded. Now she remembered. Captain Tench had been good to her aboard the convict transport bound for Botany Bay. When her baby, Charlotte was born, he had visited her soon afterward, and brought some small gift. A soldier, a lobsterback by trade, but a decent man.

Captain Tench stood beside Mary Bryant on the deck of *Gorgon* and slowly talked. He expressed his sorrow about her loss, but it would do no good to dwell on that. Could she tell him about the voyage that she and Will Bryant and the others had made in the boat? He considered it to be a very fine exploit, and during his leave at home in England he might write something about it.

Mary Bryant talked in a low, almost inarticulate voice at first, but then it became firm, and clear. Death could not destroy what had been done in the boat, she understood. Death only showed that the bravery shouldn't have been wasted.

Captain Tench bowed to Mary Bryant as he left. He said that he would be back again to visit with her. When he mounted to the quarterdeck he recalled a conversation he had heard there. Mrs. Captain Parker, whose husband commanded the ship, had been in talk with some of the New South Wales Corps wives. She had spoken tenderly of her five-year-old daughter at home. But neither Mrs. Parker nor any of the other women aboard *Gorgon* had gone to comfort Mary Bryant. Mercy in this ship was without meaning.

Mary Bryant was brought to trial in July, 1792, in London. The Bow Street magistrates had been notified of the arrival of *Gorgon* and sent for the prisoners. The five convicts called to be tried were rowed ashore in the Thames and taken to Newgate Prison. They were, according to the prison register, Will Allen, John Butcher, Nathaniel Lilly, James Martin, and Mary Bryant, alias Broad. Their crime was described: "Transports found at large before the expiration of sentence." Mary Bryant was held in Newgate as a "convict at large."

But then, in the spring of 1792, she and the rest gained a powerful friend in James Boswell, the Scottish barrister and writer. He had read about them in the newspapers and gone to interview them in the awful conditions that existed at Newgate. Boswell appealed the sentences of all five convicts, and in the case of Mary Bryant was successful.

Boswell was greatly impressed by her. He supplied her with money after she was pardoned, and paid for her passage home to Fowey in the schooner *Anne and Elizabeth*. His arrangement was that she would receive ten pounds a year from him and, because she had not yet learned to write, he taught her to sign "M. B." as receipt for the payments that were sent each half year.

Boswell did not see her again once she had returned to

Fowey. But he wrote of her at length in his journal. Captain Watkin Tench of the Royal Marines wrote of her also, and out of a full memory of what she and her husband and the others with them had performed during the voyage to Timor. The captain lacked Boswell's literary polish, still he could be eloquent:

"They had miscarried in a heroic struggle for liberty after having combated every hardship and conquered every difficulty."

Mary Bryant might have been told of the captain's account, published as a book. But she was content to remain wholly obscure in Fowey where the seas clashed black against the cliffs and at night she heard the winds which had cast her away on Timor, and finally brought her home.

Fire at sea, shipwreck, threats from pirates, voyages in small craft during the typhoon season were common in the life of this man. Peril in almost any form had been constant for Alfred Russel Wallace ever since he was a young man and went to the headwaters of the Amazon to begin his career as an ornithologist and naturalist.

Then, for eight years he cruised the reef-littered, narrow seas around the Malay archipelago, and survived to become almost as well recognized for his scientific work as his great contemporary, Charles Robert Darwin.

ALFRED RUSSEL WALLACE

SOME of Alfred Russel Wallace's first memories were of the River Usk, in his native Monmouthshire. They were to remain distinct through all of the maze of exotic circumstances and extraordinary adventures of his later life. He recalled vividly the stocky Welsh fishermen as they passed the cottage his family occupied and went down the river bank. Each man easily balanced his own boat on his back. These boats were the famous Welsh coracles, and the boy was told by his father that they had been in use since Roman times, perhaps as far back as the Neolithic age.

When Wallace came to manhood, he smiled in recollection of his father's statement. He was born on January 8, 1823, in the cottage at Usk, and the family moved from there to London before he was five. He had been quite small to be told about Roman times and the Neolithic age.

The coracles, though, were remarkable craft. They were made of strong wicker-work and resembled in shape the deeper half of a cockle shell. Bullock hide, carefully cut and stitched, then greased, was the hull covering. The fishermen paddled methodically along the river and caught fine, plump trout, salmon, and lampreys. Wallace could remember later many craft from the far parts of the world where he had sailed, and there was none like the coracle.

He had other happy memories of his youth. But over them was the massive shadow of the family's poverty. His father, Thomas Vere Wallace, was a proud, weak, and badly confused man with a wife and six children to support and a very faint idea of how he should do it. He was qualified as Attorney-at-Law of the King's Bench, and claimed that he was related to the famous Wallace clan. But he ended up teaching school wherever he could find half a dozen scholars whose parents would pay him. Debt rode higher against his best efforts, and he could provide for his family in only a miserable way. His wife's small marriage settlement was the one regular source of income. He took the family to Hertford from London in a further desperate attempt to make a living.

Alfred Wallace survived the poverty, the meanness and inevitable family bickering with a stoicism he retained all of his life. He was six feet tall when he was sixteen, and good at cricket and rugby. Scholastic ability had got him a full scholarship at the Blue Coat School in Hertford, a branch of the extremely rigorous school system maintained by Christ's Hospital and based in London. The boys wore long blue coats, yellow petticoat pants, yellow stockings, and red belts. Classes were long and the masters demanding, but Wallace learned thoroughly English grammar, Greek and Latin, and mathematics.

It was the last of his formal education. His family began to disintegrate during the years at Hertford. He left with memories of the local rivers, the Lea and the Breame, where he rowed, swam, and fished. Poverty took him to London, where he joined his elder brother, John, who was nineteen and apprenticed to a master builder.

This was early in 1837, during an age when apprentices were supposed to be confined to their quarters after darkness. But the brothers were excellent workmen, and were given permission to go into the city. They spent most of their evenings in the "Hall of Science" at John Street, in Tottenham Road.

It was a combination of a workers' club and a so-called "mechanics institute" where "advanced free-thinkers" gathered. Alfred Wallace read the papers and the pamphlets which expounded the views of Robert Owen, the founder of the nascent socialist movement in England, and was keenly stirred by Thomas Paine's doctrine in *Age of Reason*. But he was not prepared to serve any further as an apprentice in London, and in the summer of 1837 he went to work with another of his older brothers, Will, in Bedfordshire.

Will Wallace had set himself up as a land surveyor in the market town of Barton. When Alfred became his partner and pupil, they lodged at the inn and ranged all over the west of England and Wales after jobs. Alfred gradually learned celestial navigation through the use of surveying instruments, and walking the moors with the chain and rod of his trade, started to learn geology and botany, made his first collection of beetles.

He came of age in January, 1844, and decided that he should do a great deal more with his life. His father was dead, his mother a housekeeper, and his sister gone to Georgia in the United States to become headmistress of a girls' school. Wallace continued his study of botany and taught school evenings at the Free Library in Neath.

He met Henry Walter Bates, the entomologist, at the library in Leicester one night, and the men were soon friends. They read together and discussed at length an account of the South American jungle. It was *A Voyage up the Amazon* by W. H. Edwards, and they decided that they must go to Brazil as naturalists.

They sold their private botanical collections to get passage money, and in London met Edwards, and were given advice by officials of the Royal Museum. All of their spare funds went to the purchase of books, apparatus, and the necessary outfits. They practiced the shooting and skinning of birds, and then left for Liverpool and the ship that was to take them to Brazil.

She was the 192-ton bark *Mischief*, and made the run from the Mersey to Para in twenty-nine days. Wallace was greatly excited when he went ashore with Bates. This was a world almost entirely different than that he had known in England. He eagerly examined and then listed in the first of his Brazilian notebooks all of the native growths, the palms, the calabash and gourd, the orange trees, and the bananas and mangoes; and the fruits, the vegetables, even the *piassaba*, palm fiber brooms used for sweeping the streets.

Wallace and Bates decided in Para that they should separate, each seek to explore his own region in the Amazonian vastness. Wallace was fascinated by the stories told of the western tributary rivers that fed the Amazon. He moved inland toward the distant Andean watershed and the spine of the entire South American continent.

His notebooks were rapidly filled. He sketched while daylight lasted, and afterward by the light of the campfire. There were monkeys smaller than squirrels that spent their lives in the tops of trees, and monkeys as big as sheep dogs that were called red howlers. The birds seemed countless, and among them were toucans and trogans and tanagers, and the umbrella bird, the bell bird, the scarlet ibis and the roseate spoonbill.

There was a large fish called *pirarucú*, which sometimes was four feet long, and the *piranha*, with a mouth like a shark and an evil reputation as a killer. Wallace sweated enormously under the terrific, direct rays of the equatorial sun, survived his first bouts of fever, and at Barra* decided that he would go on, upriver.

Barra was a fort maintained by the Portuguese at the head of regular navigation, built high on the muddy bank of the Rio Negro twelve miles above the juncture of the Negro with the Amazon. It was also a trading post, and a hangout for a number of very strange and dangerous characters. Some of these pistol-hung men warned Wallace not to go any farther inland. They described deadly snakes, boa constrictors and bushmasters, and the cannibalistic Indian tribes, jaguars, pumas, fire ants.

Wallace disregarded the barroom warnings. His plans were already made to go up the Negro, in itself a mighty river. He had learned to speak *lingao-geral*, the common language of the Brazilian tribes. His skill with a rifle was almost flawless, and he would have no trouble gathering specimens. He was competent in a canoe, and could take his place at a paddle all day long. There were Indians whom he trusted to serve him as guides, and the Portuguese commandant had given him permission for the trip. The commandant added that the men who expressed warning to Wallace were upriver traders, hunters, and slave-runners who wanted to keep the Negro to themselves.

* Present-day Manaus.

Wallace had been enormously impressed by the Amazon. He envisioned it as the greatest of all rivers. It drew upon the rivers that stretched beyond for 3,000 miles, and down from the Andes, 1,200 miles away. The tributaries reached ancient Inca country past the Peruvian frontier, the silver mountains of Potosi, and the never-found El Dorado. The Amazon lay surrounded by Venezuela, Colombia, Ecuador, Peru, Bolivia, and Brazil. The territory it drained was much larger than Europe, and was practically unknown.

But the Negro cast a peculiar spell on Wallace. He went from it up what he called "a great river," the Uapés. That took him toward the headwaters of the Orinoco and the jungle wilderness along the Venezuelan frontier. Wallace used his sextant and compass to establish his position. He detailed landmarks, measured distances, and heights of mountains and waterfalls. This, he knew, was country rarely if ever entered by white men.

Here, along the rapid-flowing, whirling river, he met what he described as "the true denizens of the forest." The local Indian tribe had existed wholly unchanged for hundreds of centuries. Women went naked except for woven palm fiber garters. Men were oddly feminine. They wore their hair neatly parted in the middle and combed behind the ears. It was tied behind the head in a long tail that fell a yard in length over the back. The tail was firmly bound with a very soft and pliable cord made of monkey hair. They decorated the tops of their heads with combs cleverly fashioned from palm wood, each ended bedecked with feathers taken from the rumps of toucans.

The warriors had their ears pierced. Pieces of straw were thrust through the holes. They plucked their eyebrows and their beards, and adorned themselves with palm fiber gee-strings, and garters.

All of the tribe lived in a big, shedlike hut. It was solidly built of palm thatch. The chief and his wives and children maintained their quarters in the middle.

Wallace spent four years along the Rio Negro and its tributaries. He made two descents to Barra, and once found more than twenty letters waiting for him, several over a year old. They were from London, and from California, and Australia. He answered them, and went back in 1850 for another year's stay in the interior.

He carried all his valuable belongings in closely shut tin boxes, including his watch, his sextant and prismatic compass. He had with him also boxes for his insect and bird specimens. He kept his gun and ammunition handy at all times, and carried certain items for trade with the Indians. Among the lot were rum, salt, beads, calico, fishhooks, and coarse cotton cloth.

When he crossed the Serra de Cocoi on February 1, 1851, he took a sextant observation upriver on "an old friend." The friend was Polaris, and he got a reading that established his latitude at 1°20′ North, close to the Brazilian-Venezuelan frontier.

Then he decided to go home. He had come upon forty varieties of butterflies on the march across the frontier into the Orinoco country of Venezuela. But he was aware that he had been alone much too long, skinning birds in the early morning, collecting specimens, casting with a net for insects, then hunting with the gun, and afterward busy with the compilation of his notes and his sketchbooks.

Wallace went down the upper rivers, and then from Barra to Para, where the seagoing ships lay. He arranged for passage in the 235-ton brig *Helen,* under the command of Captain John Turner.

Helen sailed on July 12, 1852 for England. She caught

fire at sea three weeks later while homeward-bound. It was in the morning, soon after breakfast. Wallace sat in his cabin and read a book. He had just finished with a bout of malaria, felt weak and drowsy. But he rose quickly to his feet when the captain knocked on the cabin door and said, "I'm afraid the ship's on fire. Come see what you think of it."

Captain Turner and Wallace lifted up the hatch cover in the main cabin floor and peered into the lazarette and found no sign of fire. When they went forward, though, the fo'c'sle was full of smoke. The fore hatch was opened and some of the highly inflammable cargo of various kinds of tropical woods was jettisoned. Fire poured fierce heat upward from the lower part of the forehold, and in the afterhold it was worse.

A bucket brigade was formed but did not lessen the fire. An attempt to cut a hole through the bulkhead from the main cabin into the afterhold failed. Smoke swirled thickly through all of the living spaces in the ship.

Captain Turner gave the order to abandon ship. The longboat and the gig were swung outboard in the davits. Sailors with smoke-tears streaming down their cheeks brought all kinds of gear from the fo'c'sle, woolen pilot coats, and oilskins and seaboots, even shore hats. The captain took care to secure his sextant, chronometer, dividers, and charts. But Wallace found himself barely able to move as a consequence of the fever.

He made a fumbling trip to the cabin he had occupied and gathered a few notebooks, his watch, and a small tin box that contained a series of drawings. But he left all of the rest of his belongings. An apathy which he later described as inexplicable came over him, and he waited on deck for the captain's order to get into a boat.

The two boats which were lowered were in miserable shape. They needed rudders, oars, thole pins, sails, tools, marline twine, spare canvas, and sail needles. They also badly leaked. But there was still time to get the necessary equipment, and the steward found cask bungs that could be used to stop the bottom leaks. The mess was then cleaned off the floorboards—a tangle of blankets and pilot coats, pork, cheese, books, and biscuits.

It was now time to leave her. The men were assigned to their stations in the boats. Wallace went into the gig with the captain. She lay in the deep swell close to the longboat, both craft riding from lines secured aboard the ship.

They stayed alongside all night in the two boats as the ship burned. The reason for it was that another vessel might see the blaze, come alongside and take them aboard. Wallace hoped that some of the animals and birds he had collected might still be saved alive, carried to England.

The brig's cargo was raw rubber in the afterhold, and balsam, with the tropical woods in the forehold. The balsam gave a gurgling, bubbling sound when ignited, and sent orange gusts of flame aloft. The lower sails caught fire. It spread to the tarred, rope rigging. Then she was all afire, right up to her royals and her mast trucks.

The masts began to topple as the rigging collapsed. The mainmast swerved in a great, single dive into the sea. The foremast followed. Sparks showered, and the calm sea hissed.

Wallace watched the animals and the birds. Most of the monkeys burned to death. Some ran from places of safety and leaped into the middle of the fire. A few gathered on the bowsprit with the parrots, but they disappeared, and then only a single parrot was left.

The men in the longboat had tried to pull close alongside several times, but were held away by the heat. They were able to save the parrot, though, as the rope on which he sat burned through and he plopped into the sea. They gave him respectfully to Wallace.

Wallace sat holding the singed, stupefied bird on his wrist. He told himself that he would go back to England and start his writing with what he had saved from the ship. There was a considerable amount of specimens, notebooks, and sketches he had already sent home. He was much better off than this poor parrot.

Wallace passed the bird to a sailor to hold. The captain and the mate were plotting the ship's position and the nearest landfall. They wanted Wallace to confirm their navigation. He checked it with the same pencil stub and rumpled piece of paper they had used.

The approximate position where *Helen* caught fire, burned and sank was 30°30' North, 52° West as well as Wallace could figure it. The nearest landfall was Bermuda. The captain, the mate, and Wallace agreed, according to their calculations, that it was at least 700 miles away.

The wind was East, and fair. Captain Turner ordered a line passed from the gig to the longboat, so that the two boats would stay together. They hoisted sail and stood away on the course, making good time. Chunks of Gulf Stream seaweed were around them, and flying fish leapt, came tumbling aboard. Both were welcome signs—the Gulf Stream would help them make good their course, and the slender fish, broiled in the sun, were a pleasant addition to the steward's ration of biscuit and raw pork.

The day of August 9 was very hot. Wallace was already suffering from severe sunburn aggravated by salt water chafe. He crouched with his head down, shielding his eyes from the fierce refraction of light off the sea. The next day, there were heavy rain squalls. But the men's clothing, and the sails and the boats themselves were saturated with salt. The rain water that was caught was too brackish to be drunk.

Wallace sat up on the thwart and paid more attention

when birds were sighted. They were boobies and Mother Cary's chickens. Dolphins and pilot fish broke the surface close to the boat; bonito, barracuda, and shark were seen. Wallace memorized the noon position taken the day before. It had been 31°59′ North, 57°22′ West. He advanced it by dead reckoning and memorized the new position for the notes he would write later about the voyage.

With dawn of August 13, they had been in the boats for a week. Captain Turner ordered that both crews be limited to a half ration of water. But on August 15, along about five o'clock in the afternoon, the people in the gig saw the long-boat tack. Captain Turner said that he was sure a ship had been sighted.

The ship was the British brig *Jordeson*, under Captain Venables and bound from Cuba to London in mahogany, fustic, and other tropic woods. She made a slow passage home, met a furious storm, was down to very short rations when she reached Deal.

Wallace went ashore October 1, his ankles swollen by the effects of the storm, and wearing a thin calico suit. It had taken him 80 days from Para to England. He celebrated with a dinner shared by the two captains; they ate a large beef-steak apiece, and topped it off with damson tarts.

Wallace found when he returned to London that he had saved a good deal more of his work than he had originally believed. The tin box taken from his cabin in the burning ship contained careful pencil drawings of all of the species of palm trees, along with a large number of drawings of fish. These were done to scale, and accompanied by notes that described their colors, dentition, fin-rays and other characteristics.

He had sent home in 1850 a short paper on the umbrella bird, a species almost unknown to British ornithologists. It was printed in the *Zoological Society Proceedings* for that year, and brought him quite an amount of favorable comment on his work. He was inspirited when he went to live at 44 Upper Albany Street and began a paper about the headwaters of the Rio Negro, and drew from his notes a large map of the Uapés River region.

The paper was read at a meeting of the Royal Geographical Society, and the map exhibited. Then he started work on the manuscript that was to become his book *Travels on the Amazon and the Rio Negro*, and his next book, *Narrative*. He included in the first book the vocabularies of approximately 100 common words taken from the different Indian languages spoken in the Amazonian jungle.

He lived with his sister, his brother-in-law, and mother while in London, in a house near Regent's Park. But he spent a great part of his time at the Linnaean Society, the Kew Herbarium, the Royal Geographical Society, and the British Museum. When his books were published in 1853, he became very well-known and a recognized figure in his field.

Wallace realized after discussions with his fellow members in the various learned societies that his next endeavor should be the exploration of the Malay archipelago. The huge string of islands offered a naturalist an almost incredible source of specimens and knowledge, even greater than that he had discovered in South America. He made his preparations carefully for the task, and said good-bye to his family and friends. He planned to be gone for some years.

Sir Roderick Murchison, president of the Royal Geographical Society, procured for him free first-class passage aboard Peninsular and Oriental steamers to Singapore. He sailed from England aboard *Euxine* early in 1854 and left her at Cairo. Then he went overland with the rest of the steamer's passengers to Suez. They were carried across the desert in small, two-wheeled omnibuses drawn by four horses, with six people crammed in each. Wallace made note of the hundreds of camel cadavers along the road.

He arrived in Singapore in April, 1854, aboard the steamer *Bengal.* The fecund, lush, and vastly variegated Orient seized his interest at once. He was to spend eight years in the Malay archipelago. He wrote later that it "constituted the central and controlling incident of my life."

He went first to Malacca, and spent two months there. His work fascinated him, and he was careless about sun exposure, the kind of water he drank, and mosquitoes. Fever which he had not experienced so violently since the Rio Negro caught him. When he returned gaunt and yellow to Singapore, the government doctor gave him large doses of quinine for a week, and explained the need.

Wallace understood. He admitted that he had never used half enough quinine while in the Rio Negro country. Then, with a supply of medicine furnished him by the doctor, he went happily back to his work in the jungle-covered islands.

He accumulated a superb collection of butterflies in Malacca, and reported "hundreds of other new or rare insects." He gathered specimens of centipedes and scorpions, some of the scorpions nearly a foot long. He remarked the characteristics of elephants, water buffalo, and tigers. Sir James Brooke, the Rajah of Sarawak, sent him an invitation to visit, and he spent fifteen months on Borneo.

His collections were sent home by sailing ship around the Cape of Good Hope. The overland mail rates were too expensive for his limited budget. But he wrote enthusiastically to Bates, still on the Upper Amazon, "I have spent six months in Malacca and Singapore, and fifteen months in Borneo." Then he entered into long, extremely technical descriptions of his findings. One of them was, "Your glorious Erycinidae are represented by half a dozen rather inconspicuous species, and even the Lycaenidae, though more numerous and comprising some lovely species, do not come up to the Theclas of Para."

Wallace ranged almost constantly over the seas of the archipelago, from Singapore to Sumatra, Java, Timor, the Celebes, Borneo, and through scores of other islands to New Guinea. He sailed in any craft that he believed to be seaworthy, and several that were not and where he greatly risked his life.

During December, 1856, while at Macassar in the Celebes group, he decided to make a voyage far to the eastward. This would take him to the Aru Islands, off the western coast of New Guinea. The voyage was to be made in a native *prau*, and was only possible once a year because of the change in direction of the monsoon winds.

Wallace fully understood from traders in Macassar that the 1,000 mile voyage was considered perilous among the veteran native sailors. There were pirates in the area who each year ruthlessly raided the shipping, seized prisoners for ransom, and looted ashore. The entire west coast of New Guinea was populated by headhunters and cannibals, and they often visited the Aru Islands in their big war canoes, traded if they felt like it, or murdered the inhabitants who had not fled inland. The Aru people themselves were mop-headed and wild, famous in a fight.

Still, Wallace was determined to go. The trade between Macassar and Dobbo, the principal town in the Aru Islands, had existed since very early times. Chinese and Bugis merchants conducted most of it, sent the *praus* out in December or January, at the beginning of the west monsoon. The return passage was made in July or August, with the full strength of the east monsoon. Pearls, mother-of-pearl, and tortoise shell went from Dobbo through the hands of traders to Macassar, then to Singapore, and Europe. Sea slugs, called *tripang* in

Malay, and a great delicacy in China, were also bought and shipped, along with birds' nests.

Wallace chose to take passage in a *prau* owned by a young Javanese half-caste who warned him they would be away at sea for six or seven months. He would accept no fixed sum from Wallace, and told the Englishman to pay him whatever he saw fit when they came back from the voyage. The vessel was one of the biggest making the run to Dobbo. But they met rough weather on their first day at sea, December 13, lost the boat they towed astern, damaged their sails, and were forced to put back into port.

Wallace was very curious about the vessel. She was built on the general plans of a Chinese junk, weighed around 70 tons, and was of teak construction. Her two masts carried rattan sails, poorly rigged and hard to handle. There were double rudders, set on the quarters of the vessel and not fully astern. These were controlled by long tillers and rattan slings. The two steersmen were under the direct command of a man called a *juragan*, which Wallace translated as chief mate.

The vessel had been at sea for several days with her crew of thirty and a number of passengers aboard before Wallace discovered her amazing unseaworthiness. So that the pair of tillers could swing the rudders, large portholes had been cut in the shipside. These were less than four feet above the waterline. Any moderate sea could slop through them into the hold. Wallace had fondly believed that there was a watertight bulkhead between the hold and the cabin space in the after part of the *prau*. He was wrong. No such bulkhead existed, the captain said. But vessels like this had been built for a very long time. They should be seaworthy.

Wallace accepted the danger as another to be met and resigned himself. But he lay awake often at night and counted the waves that came sloshing through the tiller ports. Six big ones, he knew, would start to sink her. Ten would take care of her for good.

Wallace had become an excellent seaman during his many voyages. When the *prau* encountered heavy storm and the long main boom cracked with the weight of the clumsily rigged sail, he helped in the work of repair. The owner, the captain, the mates, and sailors all showed him their respect. The quiet, bespectacled Englishman was a much different person than they had first thought.

With stops at various islands along the course, the *prau* made the passage to Dobbo. Birds of Paradise, the most valuable specimen an ornithologist could find, had been brought here from New Guinea and exchanged in barter by the natives. Wallace looked carefully for more of them, aware that the pair the great naturalist Carolus Linnaeus, had seen came from this region.

It was impossible, though, for Wallace to leave Dobbo. Pirates were raiding through the island group. Vessels arrived in port almost every day with crew members missing or word of burned villages and demands for ransom. The Dutch governor prohibited all ship movement.

Wallace contented himself with hunting for insects and birds in the jungle behind the town. He was fascinated, too, by the daily scenes in the bazaar. Dobbo was really a frontier outpost; beyond it, to the east and to the north, were the savage, headhunter tribes. They came by canoe, catamaran and *prau* to barter with the traders, a mixed lot of Chinese, Bugis, Ceramese, and Javanese.

Each palm-thatch shack was a store where the out-island people bartered their goods for what they needed. Knives, swords, cleavers, guns, plates, basins, handkerchiefs, sarongs, and calico were displayed; and looking glasses, razors, umbrellas, pipes, and tobacco. Arrack, the powerful wine made from palm juice or rice, was sold, and salt, and biscuit, and tea.

Wallace strolled among the shacks, making careful notes of what he saw and heard. He watched the cock fights held in the middle of the muddy street, and the soccer matches played with a small rattan ball. He talked with the captains of vessels who had fought against the pirates, and with Chinese merchants who wore immaculate white jackets and blue trousers, red silk ribbons plaited into the queues which reached almost to their heels.

He was impatient to get out of Dobbo and along the wild, uninhabited stretches of the Aru coast. His understanding was that the Aru islanders shot the Bird of Paradise with a dull-pointed arrow. This only stunned the bird, did not harm the plumage or the bone structure, furnished a perfect specimen.

Permission to leave was finally granted Wallace, and in the middle of March, 1857, he shoved off in a small *prau* he had outfitted. He took personal command of her and cruised the coast with a native crew none of whom spoke English. He spent from March to May in exploration of Aru, and found a number of valuable specimens, among them Birds of Paradise. But his boat was grounded many times, and almost wrecked. He lost anchors and sails that could not be replaced, suffered from fever, boils, and a severe case of sunburn.

He went back to Dobbo and waited for the departure of the big trading *prau* that had taken him from Macassar. When his health was restored, he kept busy making notes, sketches and drawings. Dobbo still fascinated him, and he promised his friends there that he would see them again.

But, first, he went on other voyages of exploration far to the westward. He cruised around the island of Batchian and in the Moluccas. His base in the Moluccas was Ternate, where he had been given the use of a half-ruined house on a hilltop near the port.

It was at Ternate in 1858, just after return from a long and exhausting voyage, that Wallace came upon his conception of the theory of the evolution of species. He suffered from the intermittent fever, and spasms shook him until the rattan cot on which he lay almost collapsed. Then he shuddered with crippling, numbing chills.

Still, he was able to keep his mind clear above the pain. He recalled once more what he had learned during his years of field work in the islands of the archipelago. Charles Robert Darwin was his greatest correspondent, and Wallace recognized now that Darwin's theory of survival of the species, written twenty years before, was absolutely correct. His own thinking, reached independently of Darwin, confirmed it in every respect.

While he lay here buffeted by the fever, Wallace asked himself a series of questions. Why do some animals live, and some die? The answer was: those who were best-fitted for survival lived. The most healthy escaped from the effects of disease; the strongest, the swiftest and most cunning conquered their enemies; the best hunters, or those with the best digestions, stayed alive through famine. So it went on, through all of the species.

This self-acting process improved the race, because in every generation the inferior would certainly be killed off, and only the superior would remain. It meant survival of the fittest. This explained, as further proof of the theory, the definite characteristics and the clear isolation of each new species. Wallace had seen the differentiation of species many times as he moved from island to adjacent island in the archipelago.

Not yet free from the fever, he memorized exactly what

he was going to write. He got up when he was barely able to walk and went to his writing table. It was after sundown, and he fumbled to light the lamp, and to bring pen, ink, and paper within reach.

He worked on the subject all of that evening and the next two evenings. He wanted the paper and the letter that accompanied it to go to Darwin in the mail that was almost ready to leave. They were finished in time, and he went down into the town and gave the bulky envelope to the Dutch courier. Then he returned to the house, and to bed.

Darwin received the paper in London in 1858 and sent it along with his own work on the subject as a joint communication to the Linnaean Society. There was bitter dispute over the validity of the theory among scientists and the clergy. But Darwin remained steadfast in his praise and support of Wallace, stated repeatedly that Wallace had come upon his own private solution. The dispute gradually subsided, and the theory was accepted as a brilliant advance in scientific knowledge.

But Wallace stayed at his field work in Malaysia for four more years before he went home to England. He bought and outfitted his own boat, and in her made a voyage to Goram and Waigiou, islands north of Ternate. Tidal waves caused by volcanic disturbance rushed across the sea while the craft was offshore at night and almost sank her. The anchor cable chafed through with the severe strain from the waves, and parted. The anchor was lost; there was no other aboard. The wind took Wallace and his native crew out to sea despite all they could do with her sails and oars.

But they were able to check her motion finally as she drifted past a submerged reef. Wallace improvised an anchor. He filled a cotton sack with stones taken from the ballast. Then he secured a rope to the sack, slid the sack overboard. It held among the coral heads of the reef, and with dawn, the wind and tide right, Wallace wearily brought the boat back to land.

Wallace was again in bad physical shape when he returned to Ternate. The record of the last few months convinced him that he was ready to leave the archipelago and go home to England. He made notes of the voyage just completed.

During it, the first crew he hired deserted without warning, left him cast away on an isolated beach. Two men from the next crew were, because of adverse weather conditions, forced to stay for a month on a desert island. The boat went dangerously aground ten times on coral reefs. Four anchors were lost. The sails were devoured by rats. The small boat that was used as a tender and towed astern was lost. They were thirty-eight days on the homeward-bound passage which should not have taken more than twelve. Many days were spent without food of any kind. And homeward-bound there was no oil for the compass light. The voyage, supposedly made in the favorable season, had not offered a single day of fair weather.

Wallace ended the report: "We were always close braced up, always struggling against wind, tide, and leeway, and in a vessel that would scarcely sail nearer than eight points from the wind. Every seaman will admit that my first voyage in my own boat was a most unlucky one."

Wallace left on December 29, 1862, for England. He returned to find himself famous. He was surprised and felt quite uncomfortable. The years in the South American jungle and at sea and in the wild islands of the Malay archipelago, spent almost entirely among primitive people, had made him shy. He got out of London as soon as he could, retired to a very quiet part of Dorsetshire to put his specimens in order, arrange his sketchbooks and notebooks, and write.

BIBLIOGRAPHY

ANTHONY, IRVIN, *Ralegh and His World*, Charles Scribner's Sons, New York, 1934

BROOKS, VAN WYCK, *The Flowering of New England*, 1815–1865, Dutton & Co., Inc., New York, 1937

BYRON, HON. JOHN, *The Narrative of the Honourable John Byron*, written by himself, S. Baker & G. Leich, London, 1780

BYRON, Lord ALFRED, *The Complete Poetical Works of Byron*, Houghton, Mifflin, Boston, 1905

DAMPIER, WILLIAM, *A Voyage to New Holland*, Argonaut Press, London, 1839

DEFOE, DANIEL, *Robinson Crusoe*, London, 1719

Dictionary of American History, Scribner's, 1940

EXQUEMELIN, ALEXANDRE OLIVIER, *History of the Buccaneers of America*, Mussey, Boston, 1853

FISKE, AMOS K., *The West Indies*, G. P. Putnam's Sons, New York, 1899

HARING, C. H., *The Buccaneers in the West Indies in the 17th Century*, Methuen & Co., Ltd., London, 1910

HAWKESWORTH, JOHN, *An Account of the Voyage Undertaken by the Order of His Present Majesty for Making Discoveries in the Southern Hemispheres, and Successfully Performed by Commodore Byron, Captain Wallis, Captain Carteret and Captain Cook, in the* Dolphin, *the* Snow *and the* Endeavour; *drawn up from the journals which were kept by the several commanders, and from the papers of Joseph Banks, Esq.* London, 1773

HUME, MARTIN, *Sir Walter Ralegh*, T. Fisher Unwin, London, 1897

LEA, CHARLES HENRY, *The Inquisition in the Spanish Dependencies*, Macmillan, New York, 1922

MAYOUX, JEAN JACQUES, *Melville*, Evergreen Profile Book 9, Grove Press, Inc., New York, 1960

MUMFORD, LEWIS, *Herman Melville*, Harcourt, Brace, New York, 1929

PACK, S. W. C., *The Wager Mutiny*, Alvin Redman, London, 1964

PARR, CHARLES MCKEW, *Jan Van Linschoten*, T. Y. Crowell, New York, 1964

PECK, ANNE MERRIMAN, *The Pageant of South American History*, Longman's Green, New York, 1947

RAWSON, GEOFFREY, *Pandora's Last Voyage*, Harcourt, Brace & World, Inc., New York, 1964

ROGERS, CAPTAIN WOODES, *A Cruising Voyage Around the World*, London, 1712

ROWSE, A. L., *The Elizabethans and America*, Harper Brothers, New York, 1959

VEER, GERRIT DE, *The Three Voyages of Willem Barents to the Arctic Regions*, Printed for the Hakluyt Society, London, 1876

WALLACE, ALFRED RUSSEL, *The Malay Archipelago*, Macmillan & Co., Ltd., London, 1922

WALLACE, ALFRED RUSSEL, *My Life*, Dodd, Mead, New York, 1905

WILGUS, A. CURTIS, *Hispanic America*, Farrar & Rinehart, New York, 1941

WILLIAMSON, JAMES A., *The Age of Drake*, A. & C. Black, London, 1938

INDEX

ABOUT THE AUTHOR:

ROBERT CARSE went to sea in the American merchant marine at seventeen and for the next forty years, spent as much time on the water as he did on land. During World War II he was a survivor of the ill-fated Murmansk convoy run of May, 1942. Mr. Carse says that this experience provided perhaps the most vivid memory of his life. "We fought right among the icebergs. The huge Arctic bears, some white, some brown, crouched in terror along the ledges of their caves while we fought." This background gave him good insight into Willem Barents' trials with bears and icebergs, related in THE CAST-AWAYS. .

On land, Mr. Carse is a practiced and well-known writer. He is the author of eight novels, ten juvenile books, and ten works of nonfiction including *The Age of Piracy, Rum Row, The Moonrakers, The Seafarers,* and the recently published *The Twilight of Sailing Ships.*

Mr. Carse and his wife live in a 1762 Saltbox on Shelter Island, off Long Island.